THE SIGN OF YOUR COMING?

THE SIGN OF YOUR COMING?

By

Robert Young

Copyright © 2008 by Robert Young

All scripture quotations are from the New American Standard Version by the Lockman Foundation. (Unless otherwise noted)

All rights reserved. No part of this book may be reproduced, stored, or transmitted by any means—whether auditory, graphic, mechanical, or electronic—without written permission of both publisher and author, except in the case of brief excerpts used in critical articles and reviews. Unauthorized reproduction of any part of this work is illegal and is punishable by law

I give permission for individuals to copy the Charts for Bible study purposes.

ISBN: **978-0-615-24985-8**

Library of Congress Control Number: **2008906882**

Dedication

I wish to dedicate this book to my dear personal friends Scott and Catherine Williams. We first met in Jerusalem when they were on tour with a church group. On the last day of their tour I joined the group to introduce them to the Micah and Shoshanna Harrari, makers of Biblical Harps and my friend Reuven Prager (of Beged Ivri) maker of biblical clothing.

It did not take long for our friendship to progress as we had similar church back grounds, the same alma mater, attend the same church, and have a strong desire to know God's plan. Scott is a minister of the gospel and a trial lawyer. Catherine is an excellent bible teacher.

I cannot express my gratitude enough for the help and encouragement they have been to me over the years and more recently their editing of this book. Scott wrote the Pre-Foreword in the third person but the words apply to him as well. I do not consider our friendship a coincidence but give the glory and the thanks to our heavenly Father for our closeness and for this book. Everyone needs close friends may God bless you all with the same.

CONTENTS

Foreword xi
Preface xiii
Introduction 1
America and Britain in Prophecy 5
    Where did they come from? 6
    Where did they Go? 8
Signs before the Rapture 13
    Seven Churches 13
    Seven Seals 15
    Second Seal 17
    Third Seal 17
    Fourth Seal 18
    Fifth Seal 19
Signs Immediately before the Rapture 21
    Sixth Seal 22
    Dispensational Changes 23
    Signs in the Sun 24
    Signs in the Moon 26
    War Before the Rapture 28
    Signs In the Stars 32
    Another View of Solar and Lunar Eclipses 34

The Rapture	**39**
Explanations of Terms	**43**
The Beast with Seven Heads	46
Ten Kings	47
Present Day / Summary	48
Antichrist	49
The Eighth Beast	51
Gog the Spirit King	52
What is an Imam?	54
The 12th Imam	55
Who is the 12th Imam?	55
The 12th Imam: Why is this Especially Important Now?	57
Mystery Babylon	58
The Tribulation - Seven Trumpets	**63**
Wrath of the Lamb	63
Sign of Coming Woe's	67
Woe 1	67
The Great Tribulation	**71**
Wrath of Satan	71
The Seventh Beast	73
The Abomination	74
Wrath of Man - Woe 2 -The Eighth Beast	77
Reign of the Eighth Beast	78
Wrath of God - Woe 3	**83**
The Judgment of the Harlot	85

Days of Awe – Feast of Trumpets 87
Days of Joy - Feast of Tabernacles 91
The Millennial Reign 93
After the Millennium 95
    Conclusion 95
    Chart A 97
    Chart B 98
    Chart C 99
    Chart D 100
    Chart E 101
    Hebrew Calendars 102
Notes 103

FOREWORD

This booklet is the culmination of years of study and meditation in God's prophetic word. I grew up in a conservative non-denominational congregation of God's people. That congregation, and indeed our entire denomination, tried to consistently "speak where the bible speaks, and be silent where the bible is silent." We wanted to do things in bible ways and call things by bible names. I was trained in the verbal and plenary inspiration of the scriptures. Thus, I sincerely believe that every word (and every silence) proceeds from the mouth and mind of almighty God.

I also believe the scriptures, when properly interpreted; present a consistent non contradictory whole. We serve a God who created the universe and everything that was in it by the power of his Word. We serve a God who is a God of design and order. We serve a God who stands outside of time, and knows the end from the beginning. He is the Alpha and the Omega, the First and the Last, the beginning and the end. These are the irrefutable premises upon which my entire spiritual life has been built, and upon which all of the writings are based.

Nevertheless, may I say I also grew up in a camp of God's people that was strongly Amillennial. At some point in my spiritual journey, through personal study and meditation and through association with believers with a different eschatological perspective, It occurred to me that the Amillennial and/or preterist perspectives of beloved people of the church of my childhood, stood at odds with their stated goal of "speaking where the bible speaks and being silent where the bible is silent. The preterist and Amillennial perspectives followed by the vast majority of those believers spiritualize a large portion of the prophetic and eschatological writings of the Old and New Testaments. It occurred to me, that perhaps I should approach these writings from another perspective. I therefore dove into them applying the assumption that God says what he means, and means what he says. I attempted to understand the prophetic and eschatological scriptures (in as much as possible) literal terms. In doing so, I found myself more and more closely aligned with a great body of believers now sometimes disparagingly referred to as dispensationalists, and who perhaps more often identify themselves as Premillennial.

I believe that God lay it on my heart that I should share my spiritual journey in these scriptures, my observations and conclusions with the overall body of believers. That is the reason for this book. I hope that it blesses you.

PREFACE

This is a synopsis of writings I have done over the years. I intend to show the continuity of God's plan of redemption by exploring the various ways He has taught us this plan. The God of creation is a God of order. He is also a God of revelation. God spoke order into existence, and caused His servant to write down the record of His activity and plan past, present and future. You will find God has laid out His plan in a detailed chronological order. He expects us to study and understand and participate in that plan. The following are key elements of my conclusions and scriptural references to support them.

1. The seven Feasts of God reveal the whole plan of man's redemption through Christ. Rapture is necessarily inferred since the summer and fall harvests are yet to be fulfilled (Leviticus 23).

2. Prophecies and similitudes (likenesses, similarities) are major tools utilized in this study. God declared,

"I have also spoken by the prophets, and I have multiplied visions, and used similitudes." (Hosea 12:10).

The word similitude references "comparison or resemblance. In fact, the introduction to the book of Hosea is a parable of God's "marital relationship with Israel. It explains how God was forced to divorce Israel when she went "whoring after false gods and idols, and how God longs for healing in that relationship, and promises restoration of the relationship. Similarly, I believe the Old Testament book of Joshua is a prototype of the work of Jesus among his people (his incarnation and entry to this earth (the entry into Canaan), his rejection, the extension of grace to uncircumcised gentiles (see the salvation of Rahab the harlot), the rapture (see Jericho) and tribulation (see the seven years of warfare required to take the land). (See Similitudes, Chart C, at the end of this book.)

3. Jesus' sermon on the Temple Mount in Luke 21 describes events leading up to the rapture. Later that same evening on the Mount of Olives, Jesus told four of his apostles the rest of the story, from the great tribulation to His triumphant reign on earth; again revealing the whole plan (Mark 13, Matthew 24–25).

4. The book of Revelation is likewise laid out in chronological order. I believe the letters to the seven churches provide an overview of church history from the establishment of the church on the first Pentecost after Christ's death, to the rapture of the Philadelphia church, through the tribulation church of Laodicea (see Revelation 2, 3).

5. The "Seven Seals focus on the 100 plus years of signs and events that will culminate with the rapture of the Church. (See Chart A)

6. The "Seven Trumpets" describe what will occur during the tribulation. The Trumpets are divided into four major movements: first the wrath of the lamb; then the wrath of Satan; then the wrath of man (Revelation 8, 9); and, finally, with Seven Bowls of God's Wrath.

Then the seventh angel sounded; and there were loud voices in heaven, saying, the kingdom of the world has become the kingdom of our Lord and of His Christ; and He will reign forever and ever (Revelation 11:15) (See Chart A).

7. I am careful to let the Bible define the meaning of terms used in the bible and careful to identify the primary lesson presented by the context first. As you read this synopsis and booklet you will note that all my conclusions are backed up by specific scriptural references. There was never any need to apply hyperbolic (non-literal) language to the interpretation. On the contrary, every scripture has a literal and objective common sense meaning and interpretation.

INTRODUCTION

As noted in the foreword, I have concluded/believe the Seven Churches of Revelation 2 and 3 are both literal historic churches to which the Revelation letter was circulated, and literal historic periods of church history. In other words, they stand for seven prophetic church "ages (generations). There is every reason to believe that we are presently living in the age of the Philadelphia church, also known as the church of the open door. Never before in all of history have there been the unlimited opportunities to proclaim the gospel throughout the world that have existed since the creation of the printing press, the advent of fast, convenient and relatively inexpensive mass transit, the invention of radio, the telephone, television, and now the internet. There literally is no "iron curtain strong enough to prevent penetration of the gospel into even the darkest and most remote areas of the world.

Before going further I would like for you to note the Sardis church, the period just before the Philadelphia church age, there was no praise for the Sardis church generation. Rather, the Christians of the Sardis church and the Sardis generation are known as a "dead church," and are condemned for their divisive behaviors. This sin of division is still of course alive and well today. I so concede. It has always existed, and did not die out with the Philadelphia age. Thankfully, I have observed in my lifetime, in large part the demise of the divisive sectarian spirits that were so pervasive when I was younger, and the growth of the spirit of brotherly love which characterizes the Philadelphia age. It appears that there are fewer and fewer Pharisaical holdouts, confirming that one of Jesus' very last prayers, for oneness among his followers, is finally being fulfilled.

In man's desperation to master his own destiny he slips deeper into anarchy. Nevertheless within man there exists an inherent belief there must be a higher power. For the unbeliever that innate understanding is often expressed as a rebellious spirit against that Power. This belief results in the need for a Messiah –like figure or Savior (or the preparation for one) and/or the anticipation of a coming one. Islam anticipates divine savior, the Mahdi, who will appear at the "End of Days. Some Moslems believe it will be Mohammed ibn Hasan, the righteous descendant of the Prophet Mohammad. The theistic Jews also look for a divine Savior Messiah, and the restoration of their land where there will be righteousness and peace. Atheists rest their hopes in money and power politics (as a -material "savior). And Christians are expecting their divine savior Christ to come and gather them out of the corruption of this world and finally reign as "King over all the earth.

Can a consensus be reached concerning this higher power? I believe so! The Bible is the only book in the world that has accurately revealed historical events before they occur. The Bible contains the answers to coming events right down to the last day.

The purpose of this article is to share with you from the Bible, the sequential end time plan of God. This will include God's plan contained in His feast days, the predicted signs, and the counting of days revealed in the word of God. In Luke Jesus gave us an overview of how things would be in our day and time:

> There will be signs in sun and moon and stars, and on the earth dismay among nations, in perplexity at the roaring of the sea and the waves, men fainting from fear and the expectation of the things which are coming upon the world; for the powers of the heavens will be shaken.(Luke 21:25–26).

In response to Jesus' proclamation concerning prophetic signs in the heavens, sun, moon and stars a study was conducted to see if there was any correlation between said heavenly signs and Gods' previous establishment of Feast Days (Leviticus 23). By analyzing the numbering of days given in the Word, I was able to tie together actual dates for past and potential dates for coming events. (Chart B) I am not so bold as to think I could not be wrong in some of my applications, but at the same time neither am I so naïve as to think God does not have a revealed end time plan. At the least I hope you can appreciate the detailed plan as a possible scenario. I do not consider it double talk when we are told in 1 Thessalonians: "But you, brethren, are not in darkness, that the day would overtake you like a thief;" (1 Thessalonians 5:4).

Admittedly I am out of my comfort zone on some of the material presented; but I choose to press through the risk of being wrong for fear of not being obedient.

AMERICA AND BRITAIN IN PROPHECY

It is imperative that we know how America and Britain fit into bible prophecy, otherwise we will not be able to interpret passages that mention both names of Judah" and Israel. Therefore, before we start a chronological study of the signs before and after the rapture we must learn a biblical perspective on how the tribes of Ephraim and Manasseh fit into coming events. The answer is found in another prophecy in (Genesis 26:18). There we find Jacob (Israel) pronouncing the blessing on Joseph's sons Ephraim and Manasseh. The prophecy is that Ephraim's descendants will become a "group of nations and Manasseh will be a "great nation." It is not illogical to suggest that Ephraim is the United Kingdom of Great Britain and Manasseh is the USA. If not these nations, then who fulfills these prophecies? History confirms the involvement of these two brothers (nations) fighting for the Jews (Israel) to help fulfill the plan of God. The prophetic scriptures foretell the judgment on Esau (the Palestinians) that will be accomplished by the two sons of Joseph fighting for Jewish people of Israel (Obadiah 1:18). Jacob prophesied over all his sons and it was said of Judah, "the scepter would not depart from him (Genesis 49:10) No believer argues this prophecy. Why is it so difficult to believe the prophecies concerning Ephraim and Manasseh must also be literally fulfilled? In fact, think about all the English speaking nations and their relationship to the ten tribes. Let's believe what the scriptures say. All these prophecies are true. A Jewish Lawyer, Arnold L. Beizer, gave an excellent study on these matters in his book, If You Don't Ask You Will Never Know. i

WHERE DID THEY COME FROM?

Let's start at the beginning of the twelve tribes of Israel. Jacob had twelve sons, by four separate wives and concubines. The sons were Reuben, Simeon, Levi, Judah, Zebulun, Issachar, Dan, Gad, Asher, Naphtali, Joseph, and Benjamin. Jacob's son Joseph had two sons, Manasseh and Ephraim, which Jacob placed, on the same level as his own sons. (See Genesis 48).

Therefore, when one drops Joseph's name and replaces it with his two sons, the count is 13 tribes. However, in the distribution of the land in Joshua 13, the tribe of Levi had no share.

As one reads (Revelation 7:1-8) we find twelve tribes are mentioned and 12,000 leaders are chosen from each tribe. In naming the tribes Ephraim and Dan are missing from the 12 tribes listed in Revelation 7 and replaced with Joseph and Levi. This is only mentioned in passing, but will not be addressed in this study.

In (Genesis 48–49) we find the birth right blessing being passed from Jacob to Joseph and on to Ephraim, the youngest.

"Though Judah prevailed over his brothers, and from him came the leader, yet the birthright belonged to Joseph. (1 Chronicles 5:2).

Included in this was the giving of Jacob's name (Israel) to Ephraim and Manasseh.

> Jacob gave the double portion, the birthright blessing, to the younger son Ephraim; Joseph was upset with Jacob because the eldest son was entitled to the double portion. The birth right blessings pronounced by Jacob are founded in Genesis 48:18–20.
>
> Joseph said to his father, "Not so, my father, for this one is the firstborn. Place your right hand on his head. But his father

refused and said, 'I know, my son, I know; he also will become a people and he also will be great. However, his younger brother shall be greater than he, and his descendants shall become a multitude of nations.' He blessed them that day, saying, "By you Israel will pronounce blessing, saying," 'May God make you like Ephraim and Manasseh!' Thus he put Ephraim before Manasseh. (Genesis 48:18–20).

Then Jacob summoned his sons and said, "Assemble yourselves that I may tell you what will befall you in the days to come." (Genesis 49:1) Then Jacob summoned his sons and said, "Assemble yourselves that I may tell you what will befall you in the days to come. (Genesis 49:1).

The scepter shall not depart from Judah, nor the ruler's staff from between his feet, until Shiloh comes, and to him shall be the obedience of the peoples. (Genesis 49:10).

From the God of your father who helps you, And by the Almighty who blesses you With blessings of heaven above, Blessings of the deep that lies beneath, Blessings of the breasts and of the womb.(Genesis 49:25).

All the sons received a prophetic blessing as to what would befall their descendants in the future, some good and some bad. My point is this; did these blessings become null and void on ten of these tribes somewhere along the line? We constantly hear preaching that, **"the scepter will not depart from Judah.** However, become strangely silent in proclaiming Ephraim **"will become a group of nations.** Let us be honest, there are about 14 million Jews in the world, with about 7 million living in Israel but only 3.5 million are Jewish. By today's standard, this number hardly counts as a nation, much less a "great people or a "group of Nations". I can only think of three possibilities, a) God failed, or b) the blessing was made void through disobedience or c) it was accomplished. The first I would not consider. The second is a possibility and the third is logical and probable.

The children of Israel came out of Egypt and into the land God had promised Abraham around 1373 BC. After Solomon's death the 12 tribes divided. The 10 tribes to the north formed a Northern Kingdom called Israel and the two tribes of Judah and Benjamin made up the southern kingdom called Judah. This occurred around 931 BC. The 10 tribes of Israel were taken captive by the Assyrians in 722 BC. Given the fact that Israel was in the land for over 650 years, their population at that time should be well into the millions.

WHERE DID THEY GO?

It was over 100 years later, in 605 BC that the captivity of Judah began to take place. Their captors were the Babylonians, who had gained world power from the Assyrians around 625 BC. It was during this Babylonian captivity that the people from Judah took on the name "Jews and they are called by this name to this present day. As prophecy required, this same group retained its identity and genealogical tables, and returned to Judea 70 years later. God had promised that Messiah would be born in the Promised Land, and be a royal descendant of Judah and King David. The Messiah came as promised, and laid down his life for the sins of the world. "For God so loved the world that he gave his one and only Son, that whoever believes in Him shall not perish but have eternal life. (John 3:16).

About thirty seven years after his birth, He rose from the dead and went back to His Father, Jerusalem was destroyed (AD 70) and the final Diaspora of the Jews began. The regathering of the Jews officially started in 1948 AD when they became a nation again, by the name of Israel.

Remember that the 10 tribes of Israel over the years lost their identity, whereas the Jews never have. In spite of the persecutions, the Jews have endured through great persecution as they were run out of country after country. When the Assyrian captivity of Israel occurred some of Israel (the "ten tribes) migrated to Judah, along with most of the priestly tribe of Levi. However, millions were taken captive and relocated. In the ninth year of Hoshea, the king of Assyria captured Samaria and carried Israel away into exile to Assyria, and settled them in Halah and Habor, on the river of Gozan, and in the cities of the Medes. (2 Kings 17:6).

Some teach that Judah absorbed the 10 tribes of Israel and only a few were taken in to Assyrian captivity. This would have been physically impossible due to the large number involved. Nearly 200 years after their captivity the prophet Daniel saw it differently.

> Righteousness belongs to You, O Lord, but to us open shame, as it is this day--to the men of Judah, the inhabitants of Jerusalem and all Israel, those who are nearby and those who are far away in all the countries to which You have driven them, because of their unfaithful deeds which they have committed against You. (Daniel 9:7)

Nearly 250 years later the historian Josephus writes about this period, explaining how the tribes of Judah and Benjamin were together.ii He also wrote concerning his current time in this manner: "but the entire body of the people of Israel remained in that country; wherefore there are but two tribes in Asia and Europe subject to the Romans, while the ten tribes are beyond Euphrates till now, and are an immense multitude, and not to be estimated by number. iii God has dealt with Judah and Israel separately.

And I saw that for all the adulteries of faithless Israel, I had sent her away and given her a writ of divorce, yet her treacherous sister Judah did not fear; but she went and was a harlot also.(Jeremiah 3:8).

The Regathering of Israel "In that day, declares the LORD, "you will call me my husband'; you will no longer call me 'my master.' ----- I will betroth you to me forever; I will betroth you in righteousness and justice, in love and compassion. (Hosea 2:16–19, NIV).

And the LORD said, "Name him Lo-ammi, for you are not My people and I am not your God." Yet the number of the sons of Israel Will be like the sand of the sea, Which cannot be measured or numbered; And in the place Where it is said to them, 'You are not My people,' It will be said to them, 'You are the sons of the living God'. And the sons of Judah and the sons of Israel will be gathered together, and they will appoint for themselves one leader, And they will go up from the land, For great will be the day of Jezreel (Hosea 1:9–11).

Here we find affirmation of the promise made to Abraham, the number of Israelites will far exceed the present day 14 million. The ones that are not called my people will be called the sons of the living God (lost Israel). The Jews have always been associated with one God, Jehovah.

When we study through Ezekiel chapter 36 and 37, we discover that Ezekiel is talking about the house of Israel, meaning the "ten lost" tribes. The house of Israel is described as dried buried bones; they were totally out of sight. Then it promises that they will be brought to life and joined with Judah and the Israelites associated with him! This is saying, one day these ten lost tribes will be manifested (identified) and joined with the Jews (Judah) to make one great nation:

> The word of the LORD came again to me saying. "And you, son of man, take for yourself one stick and write on it, For Judah and for the sons of Israel, his companions; then take another stick and write on it, For Joseph, the stick of Ephraim and all the house of Israel, his companions. Then join them for yourself one to another into one stick that they may become one in your hand." When the sons of your people speak to you saying, Will you not declare to us what you mean by these? say to them, 'Thus says the Lord GOD, 'Behold, I will take the stick of Joseph, which is in the hand of Ephraim, and the tribes of Israel, his companions; and I will put them with it, with the stick of Judah, and make them one stick, and they will be one in My hand. The sticks on which you write will be in your hand before their eyes.' Say to them, 'Thus says the Lord GOD, "Behold, I will take the sons of Israel from among the nations where they have gone, and I will gather them from every side and bring them into their own land; and I will make them one nation in the land, on the mountains of Israel; and one king will be king for all of them; and they will no longer be two nations

and no longer be divided into two kingdoms." (Ezekiel 37:15–22.)

There is no way to put two items together when you can see just one. We can see the Jews in the land of Israel and we could write Judah on their stick. Nevertheless, until such a time the other stick becomes visible it will be impossible to write Ephraim on it. This will not happen until Messiah comes to earth.

SIGNS BEFORE THE RAPTURE

Lets us begin the time line of signs and prophecy. Just before Jesus was crucified he gave John a lesson on the temple Mount about the signs to watch for before His coming for the Church (Luke 21). Later that evening on the Mount of Olives (a different location), he completed that end time outline in a conversation with just 4 of His disciples present (a different audience) (Matthew 24, Mark 13). In that later conversation Jesus reminded John about the coming great tribulation prophesied by Daniel. Jesus also taught John about signs to watch for, heralding a warning of these impending events. Next Jesus spoke of the trumpet ingathering of Israel and some of the judgments that would occur when He returns to earth (Mathew 24:25).

SEVEN CHURCHES

Several years later in AD 95, John was transported to heaven to receive a more detailed revelation of the same prophecies Jesus had summarized just before His crucifixion. In Revelation 1:9–20 while John was in the spirit he found himself having a heavenly vision where he was commanded to write down everything he "sees in a book (the book of Revelation) and send it to the seven churches in Asia. Included in that book (G 975, biblion, scroll, book), John was also instructed to record and send seven special messages to seven churches in Asia (Asia Minor, now Turkey) (Revelation 2-3).

When one investigates the messages to these seven churches we find they apply not only to those specific churches, but to the church as a whole, and to each believer in the various congregations of Christians. However, I believe the primary purpose of inserting these letters was to give all Christians of all time a prophetic over view of the "history of the church. I believe the order (time period) of these seven churches represents the condition the church has or will find itself in through approximately 2000 years of church history (Pentecost to rapture). (See Chart E) This interpretation of the seven letters to the seven churches (seven being a number of His new system signifying completion and standing for <u>all</u> the churches), also demonstrates how the book of Revelation is organized. The Holy Spirit gives John an overview and then focuses in on various details, followed by, another overview and a focusing in until the whole end times plan is completed.

Most prophecy teachers believe we are presently in the time period of, the last church, of Laodicea (which means people rule) and that our church age is "Luke-warm. But I believe we are we presently the Philadelphia church and have a guarantee to be raptured before the tribulation starts.

"Because you have kept the word of My perseverance, I also will keep you from the hour of testing, that hour which is about to come upon the whole world, to test those who dwell on the earth. (Revelation 3:10).

This would make the Laodicea believers part of the tribulation church, and not part of the "bride because the time of grace will be over. Consequently believers during the tribulation will have to buy their white garments in order to share Christ's throne (Revelation 3:18–22). I believe the similitude in Joshua 9:1–16, confirms this argument. There Joshua was tricked in to a covenant with the Gibeonites and they were required to work for their standing among God's covenant people, serving as wood cutters of the temple. In like manner those that voluntarily take the mark of God during the tribulation will serve in similar manner.

Before going on I want to remind you during the Sardis church, period of history just before ours, there was no praise for them. Rather they were known as a dead church and condemned for their division.

This sin of course is alive in the church to day. But I have observed the Philadelphia church of brotherly love is being fulfilled in these last days as prophesied. With fewer and fewer Pharisaical hold outs thereby fulfilling one of Jesus' last prayers for oneness is being fulfilled.

SEVEN SEALS

After John wrote about the seven churches he looked up and saw an open door. He was invited up into the throne room and very presence of God where he would continue writing the book as God revealed truth to him through a series of visions and oral instructions about things that must take place "hear after (Revelation 4:1). In chapter 10 of Revelation John starts to write yet another section of the book, but is stopped by the Holy Spirit and required to "eat that scroll or book, and then to prophesy again as the Seventh trumpet (signaling the wrath of God) was a about to sound, and the mystery of God neared completion (Revelation 10:7).

John continues to write the book of Revelation as these prophesies were presented to him in the form of a scroll (or book, G 975) held in the hand of God and sealed with seven seals. The first six of these seals give us a sneak preview of events that take place before our Lord Jesus' return to earth for the rapture of the Church. To fully understand the mystery revealed by the seven seals, we must lay the summary which Jesus gave us in his two eschatological sermons (described in (Luke 21 and Matthew 24) side by side with the seven seals of (Revelation 6). When one conducts this exercise, he finds that Jesus' sermons are parallel and complimentary to the opening of the seven seals. The Seventh Seal reveals everything from the rapture though the 1000 year reign. This includes the seven years of tribulation and Gods plan to graft Israel back into the original olive tree, and the ultimate redemption of the Promised Land. This conclusion is to be expected because God's word is on the line.

> Therefore say to the house of Israel, 'Thus says the Lord GOD, "It is not for your sake, O house of Israel, that I am about to act, but for My holy name, which you have profaned among the nations where you went. I will vindicate the holiness of My

great name which has been profaned among the nations, which you have profaned in their midst. Then the nations will know that I am the LORD, declares the Lord GOD, 'when I prove Myself holy among you in their sight.' "For I will take you from the nations, gather you from all the lands and bring you into your own land. (Ezekiel 36:22–24).

We should not attribute this plan (that is the plan revealed in the seven seals) to anyone other than God the Father and his son the Lamb of God. It was revealed in John's heavenly encounter that 'the Lion of the tribe of Judah the Root of David has triumphed' (Revelation 5:5).

The Lamb alone was worthy to take the scroll and open its seven seals. As we progress through these seven seals I will explain that when any of these "bad guys actually accomplish anything a formulistic phrase is used, thus: power was <u>given</u> to them that is delegated influence or delegated authority. It is not until the great tribulation of Trumpets 5 and 6 that Satan is finally permitted to fully exercise his own permissive power.

The Lamb, the only one qualified, opens each seal of the scrolls and is declared to be the first and the last (Revelation 1:1). He is the kinsman redeemer to Israel, similar to Boaz in the book of Ruth. Jesus has a kingly lineage from David and the tribe of Judah, whose power and authority is everlasting (Matthew 28:18). Revelation 19:11 asserts that he rides upon a white horse when he returns to earth. Therefore, I believe Jesus is the rider of the white horse of the first seal mentioned in Revelation 6:2. For an overview of the 7 Seals, 7 Trumpets, and 7 Bowls, see Chart A. First Seal

When Jesus opens the First Seal (Revelation 6:1, Matthew 24:5), it was in preparation for battle. Jesus is seen in the text as a crowned conqueror. He gathered his army which included Judah (the Jews), his followers the Church and specifically Ephraim. "I will bend Judah as I bend my bow and fill it with Ephraim (Zechariah 9:13). This text confirms Judah as the bow and Ephraim as the arrows. There is no need to read between the lines here. It would be wise to let the scriptures speak for themselves. It is my contention that the opening of the Seals correlates to the events surrounding the establishment of the geographical nation of Israel and the return of Jews to their promised land. The reestablishment of the Hebrew language and the return of

40,000 Russians Jews to Israel (Aliyah) took place during this seal. I believe the coming of the Lord will be like it was in the days of Noah in that the preparation will take 120 years from initiation to completion (Matthew 24:37). A study of these seals and historical events supports the proposition that the first seal was opened near the turn of the 20th century. In other words, it will be 120 years from the opening of this first seal to the return of Jesus on a white horse as King of Kings and Lord of Lords. As He carries out this heavenly plan he will accomplish two things: 1) He will bring His bride to her promised mansions; (John 12:2–3). 2) He will bring Judah and Israel together as one nation (stick) in their land under His rule. God will keep his word. (Ezekiel 37:16–19).

SECOND SEAL

When the Second Seal (Revelation 6:3–4, Matthew 24:6) was opened Power was given (that is delegated influence, authority) to this rider, with a great sword, to take peace from the earth. Again using said time line and historical event, this seal correlates as WW I, "the great war" (1914–1918). As a result of WW I Britain (Ephraim) acquired the whole territory of Trans Jordan and the <u>Land was made ready</u> for the coming Jewish home land. On June 22, 1922 the League of Nations' accepted the Balfour Declaration approving the British Mandate over Palestine which gave the entire West bank (land west of the Jordan River) to the Jews for a national home land.iv We now know the full land grant was not kept, in my opinion their failure resulted in a judgment by God wherein they lost most of their kingdom over the next years. Another thing God accomplished though the British Empire was spreading the English language around the world.

THIRD SEAL

As the Third Seal (Revelation 6:5-6, Matthew 24:7) was opened a rider on a black horse with a pair of scales in his hands (representing famine) comes on the scene between WWI and WWII. 21 million people died from famine during this time frame. The famine moved from place to place but was restricted in that it could not hurt the oil and the wine. "European nations, the United States, and other developed countries have not reported any instances of famine during the 20th century." v This seal was used to realign people around the world. There was Aliyah of over 123,000 during this period. These returnees started buying up the land and Tel Aviv grew from 16,500 to over 150,000. A fifth Aliyah of 215,222 took place between 1933 and 1939. vi

FOURTH SEAL

The Fourth Seal (Revelation 6:7–8, Matthew 24:7) <u>prepared the Jews for the land</u>. The rider of this pale horse was named Death and <u>hell followed</u> and Power was given him (that is delegated influence, authority) over one fourth of the earth. I believe power of this spiritual rider is restricted to 1/4th the earth and the charge of the Third Seal to not hurt the oil or the wine are still in force during this Fourth Seal period of time. This spiritual entity were given power not to kill one fourth the population but they could use war, hunger (famine), death (other than war such as terrorism, and martyrs), and pestilences, that is diseases caused by animals such as aids caused by monkeys, over one forth the earth. The opening of this seal starts with war, which I believe was WW II. We have observed the results of this seal as it continues today in a chronological order. What I mean by this is when Jesus outlined these birth bangs in (Matthew 24 and Luke 21), they are identical and in the same chronological order as the seals. Therefore, as Jesus addresses his disciples from the Temple Mount in (Luke 21:8-11), he tells how these preliminary signs will take place first. But He makes it clear the end is not yet. In reality Jesus has told us the opening of the first four seals, (the four horses of the Apocalypse) will be the first signs we are to recognize before the rapture of the Church. Jesus drops the analogy at this point and makes it clear the end will not come immediately after these four seals are opened (Luke 21:9 and Matthew 24:6). He then inserts a teaching about the Diaspora and closes this section by saying: "for there will be great distress upon the land and wrath to this people; and they will fall by the edge of the sword, and will be led captive into all the nations; and Jerusalem will be trampled underfoot by the Gentiles until the times of the Gentiles are fulfilled." (Luke 21:23–24). Daniel makes it clear that there is a seventieth week that Israel must face (Daniel 9:24). The Gentile time of grace will end with the rapture of the Church and the clock will resume for Israel. That seventh week of Daniel is the seven years of tribulation. The clock will start ticking immediately without a gap in years as some teach.

It is interesting to note this is the only rider who has a name. Whereas the first rider is identified by description, the other riders are not identified. This rider is identified as "Death and "Hell follows later. I believe these names are generic, and they introduce two new evil spiritual leaders; which will eventually usurp the waning power of the present sixth beast, the Roman Empire (presently represented by the two feet of Daniels vision).

I will explain in more detail later why I believe the rider "Death is actually" Gog. Later we will find Gog is a warring spirit, who comes on the scene at the perfect time in history to influence WWII and the holocaust. Gog may be the rider of the pale horse of the Fourth Seal. The "Hell that follows death is the increasing satanic influence of Hades, where the antichrist will eventually arise out of the ten toes.

FIFTH SEAL

The Fifth Seal reveals souls under the altar (Revelation 6:9-11, Matthew 24:9–13). In 1967, during the six day War in Israel the old city and the Temple Mount were taken the very day as prophesied in the scriptures (see argument by Sir Robert Anderson).vii This was another sovereign act of God through the Jewish people. It gave the survivors of the Holocaust, those slain (butchered) "for the word of God and for the testimony which they held" (Revelation 6:9–10) the opportunity to go directly under the alter, at the Western wall and cry, "How long, Sovereign Lord, holy and true, until you judge the inhabitants of the earth and avenge our blood? The answer is found in verse 11:" **wait a little longer, until the number of their fellow servants and brothers who were to be killed as they had been was completed.** The Fifth Seal stimulated Jewish people to look for their Messiah and hunger for a land of their own where they would be safe and free from persecution, and could practice the tenets of their faith freely, even including the rebuilding of the Temple. Today this work is all but done, with plans will under way to rebuild the Temple.viii

SIGNS IMMEDIATELY BEFORE THE RAPTURE

In recent years we have experienced the increase of earthquakes, famines, and diseases caused by animals. We must remember these signs are likened to birth pangs. Therefore, we will see the intensity and the frequency of these natural disasters continue to increase in number and severity. Another example, when one goes to the "'National Earthquake Information Center – NEICix we can see the increase of what the NEIC calls "significant earthquakes, large noteworthy and or those with a magnitude of 7.0 or greater. Every one of the three categories, plus the number of deaths, is much higher than the previous decade. From 1991 through 2001 there were forty in the large category. In 2002 alone there were forty six with an average of fifty five per year through 2007. 2008 seems to be on schedule, with twenty five large earthquakes through May 12.

Let's now turn our attention to the rest of Luke 21 starting at verse 25. There Jesus describes specific signs to look for just before his coming for the Church. We are already seeing the signs described in verse 25. We have seen the waves roaring via the tsunamis and hurricanes. Consider the numerical increase worldwide in these disasters.

Sixth Seal

Jesus then describes the Sixth Seal, (Luke 21:25–26, Revelation 6:12–17). This is the Heavenly warning sign that the tribulation is about to start and the rapture of the church is about to take place. What can we expect to see when this event takes place? Verse 26 tells us men's hearts will fail because of this final sign we are to experience. The more detailed account of this event is in Revelation 6:

I looked when He broke the sixth seal, and there was a great earthquake; and the sun became black as sackcloth made of hair, and the whole moon became like blood; and the stars of the sky fell to the earth, as a fig tree casts its unripe figs when shaken by a great wind. The sky was split apart like a scroll when it is rolled up, and every mountain and island were moved out of their places. Then the kings of the earth and the great men and the commanders and the rich and the strong and every slave and free man hid themselves in the caves and among the rocks of the mountains; and they said to the mountains and to the rocks, "Fall on us and hide us from the presence of Him who sits on the throne, and from the wrath of the Lamb; for the great day of their wrath has come, and who is able to stand?" (Revelation 6:12–17).

Everyone, including the kings, bondsmen or free men will understand this sign which will announce the coming wrath of the Lamb. It will strike fear into the hearts of those with no understanding. But when believers see this sign, they are encouraged to "lift up your heads, because your redemption draws near (Luke 21:28). Remember disciples of Jesus today are the Philadelphia church and we have His promise from "that hour".

> Because you have kept the word of My perseverance, I also will keep you from the hour of testing, that hour which is about to come upon the whole world, to test those who dwell on the earth. (Revelation 3:10).

We will be able to observe these signs as they take place; but is there any way to anticipate when this sixth seal will be opened and what will happen when it is opened?

DISPENSATIONAL CHANGES

My studies of "dispensational changes in the Bible revealed a pattern, **I found God always gives a heavenly sign followed by a sixty day, more or less, transitional period before the start of a new dispensation.** This heavenly sign occurs on the 10th of Nissan, the 14th being Passover and the new dispensation starts on Pentecost. Therefore, according to this pattern one can expect that great sign prophesied by Jesus to occur on the 10th of Nissan and the rapture of the Church to take place on Pentecost. In fact, Israel was required to count the days "the Omer from the "Feast of First Fruits to the "Day of First Fruits (Pentecost), from the spring harvest to the summer harvest. The Church (spiritual Israel) should also count these days. After we see this heavenly sign of the Sixth Seal, we will anticipate the dispensation of grace ending and the redemption of our bodies. The transformation of our bodies will take place in a twinkling of an eye on the "Day of First Fruits (Pentecost) which is always a Sunday. Isn't that neat?

The importance of dress rehearsals and the patterns laid out in Gods feast days cannot be over emphasized. **(Chart D)** demonstrates some of the roll feast days have in God's plan, along with transition periods past and future.

The scriptures teach that Jesus fulfilled the spring harvest at the feast of "First Fruits." (1 Corinthians 15:20). The "first fruits" wave offerings at this feast **were accepted by God.** (Leviticus 23:9–14). The church and the 144,000 will fulfill the summer harvest (the second harvest) on the "Day of First Fruits (Pentecost). We know this because the only ones in the scripture called "first fruits are Jesus, the Church and the 144,000. The analogy of offerings including the two unleavened loaves of bread also confirms who these "first fruits are. These offerings are waved before God and **given to the priest** thereby being the **"first fruits to Christ** (Leviticus 23:15–22)! So the Church (His bride) is given to Jesus also the "144,000 follow the Lamb wherever He goes being first fruits to God Revelation 14:4). We will see later how Israel will fulfill the fall harvest the Feast of Trumpets.

After describing the Sixth Seal (Luke 21:25-26, Revelation 6:12–17), almost like an afterthought, Jesus gives us one more clue to help us know the time of our redemption is drawing near.

> And he spake to them a parable; Behold the fig tree, and all the trees; When they now shoot forth, ye see and know of your own selves that summer is now nigh at hand. So likewise ye, when ye see these things come to pass, know ye that the kingdom of God is nigh at hand. (Luke21:29–31 NIV)
>
> I believe Jesus is telling the Church that when you see Israel and the other nations coming together in an alliance, we are to know the summer harvest, the rapture is near. Exciting times!

Let's look at this parable of the fig tree in more detail, as Jesus placed it last, it may be the last sign we can identify before the heavenly sign of the Sixth Seal. If God takes vengeance on the Arab Muslims as I believe (see following section "War before the Rapture," Judaism and Christianity will be embolden around the world and bring about the fulfillment of prophetic scriptures. This will result in the EU rewriting their failed constitution that left God out of it. The Catholic Church will be invited to help rewrite this constitution and their roots of Christian values will be incorporated into it. Nations will be able to shake off the shackles of political correctness even to the point of requiring immigrants to conform to these values. The acceptance of this new EU constitution will be the "budding of all the trees. Christianity will flourish and the Muslim religion will be known for the evil it stands for. Israel will begin to bud and prosper in association with the EU. Israel will tear down the walls they are putting up for their protection; making way for the prophetic Magog invasion against unwalled cities of (Ezekiel 38–39, see Chart B).

SIGNS IN THE SUN

God has used the sun for signs in the past and He will in the future. The next heavenly warning sign will be just before the rapture when the Sun will be as black as sack cloth (Luke 21:25, Revelation 6:12). One third of the sun will be darkened as a heavenly warning that the great tribulation is about to start (Revelation 8:12). As a final sign via the sun there will be total darkness on the kingdom of the beast, the fifth bowl of God's wrath, warning men to repent before the return of Jesus and

Armageddon (Revelation 16:10–11). The signs in the sun will have come full circle. Just as there was darkness in Egypt before God made a covenant with the nation of Israel the same sign will take place before God receives his whoring wife (Israel) back. Prior to this total darkness the "heat from the sun scorches all mankind (Revelation 16:8–9).

Investigating, current signs of radiation from the sun I found these quotes:

> On 4 November 2003, the largest solar flare ever recorded exploded from the Sun's surface, sending an intense burst of radiation streaming towards the Earth. Before the storm peaked, x-rays overloaded the detectors on the Geostationary Operational Environmental Satellites (GOES), forcing scientists to estimate the flare's size. --Taking a different route, researchers from the University of Otago used radio wave-based measurements of the x-rays' effects on the Earth's upper atmosphere to revise the flare's size from a merely huge X28 to a "whopping" X45, say researchers Neil Thomson, Craig Rodger, and Richard Dowden. X-class flares are major events that can trigger radio blackouts around the world and long-lasting radiation storms in the upper atmosphere that can damage or destroy satellites. The biggest previous solar flares on record were rated X20, on 2 April 2001 and 16 August 1989."This makes it more than twice as large as any previously recorded flare, and if the accompanying particle and magnetic storm had been aimed at the Earth, the damage to some satellites and electrical networks could have been considerable," says Thomson. Their calculations show that the flare's x-ray radiation bombarding the atmosphere was equivalent to that of 5,000 Suns, though none of it reached the Earth's surface, the researchers say. All X-flares are major, and few have been recorded that were larger than X-10 "The fourth largest in the last 15 years, September 4, 2005, the flare was rated an X-17.x A solar outburst, which can play havoc with global positioning systems and cell phone reception, bombarded Earth, Dec. 6, 2006, with a record amount of radio noise; ---the disruption lasted more than an hour, produced a

record amount of radio noise, and caused massive disruptions of Global Positioning Satellite (GPS) receivers' worldwide.xi

It appears the signs in the sun, that Jesus asked us to look for before and after his return (Luke 21:25) may be related to "whopping solar activity.

SIGNS IN THE MOON

Just as God used the sun to warn unbelievers He uses the moon to guide believers. He used the moon for His Holy days and special events. The numbering of days and the governing of His people was based on the moon cycle of the Hebrew calendar. However, traditionally Israel believed an eclipse of the moon was a bad omen for Israel and an eclipse of the sun was bad for Israel's enemy.

In response to Jesus telling us to look for signs in the moon in Luke 21:25, I found the following list of **total lunar eclipses** that will occur on **God's feast days** over the current eight year period:

2007 March 3, Adar 14, Purim

2008 February 21, Adar 15, Shushan Purim

2014 April 15, Nisan 15, Passover

2014 October 8, Tishre 14, Succoth, Tabernacles

2015 April 4, Nisan 15, Passover

2015 September 28, Tishre 15, Succoth, Tabernacles

In 2014 and 2015 four total lunar eclipses will occur on Passover and Tabernacles -- God's Holy days each of these two years. I am not a statistician and have no idea what the odds would be on these events taking place, but it seems to me they are of biblical proportion. When one searches the internet for similar patterns, past or future none can be found. xii

These first two total eclipses take place on the fasts of Esther in 2007 and Shushan Purim 2008, both of which were celebrated as Jewish festivals during Jesus' earthly ministry. (See Chart B for possible scenario).

The first total lunar eclipse on the fast of Esther March 3, 2007 was in the longitude of Israel and was seen on every Continent. We are indeed coming into some rare eclipse patterns. This was like a shout from God to the whole world; look at the signs in the moon. Let me insert if one takes this date of March 3, 2007 and adds 7 years, 3 months and 3days you will come to the start of the next dispensation, Daniel's 70th week. There will be another total eclipse, in this time frame that I did not mention because it did not fall on a holy day. This event will take place on December 21, 2010, and based on the time line I am using (see Chart B) it takes place 1260 days before the start of the seventh week of Daniel. Are these signs coincidence or are we supposed to count down the days like Daniels seventh week?

Can we make an application on the first two eclipses? The first thing that comes to mine is these eclipses take place on Purim which celebrates how Queen Esther (meaning "I will conceal" saved the Jewish people from annihilation. The book of Esther is also a similitude of how Gog, the last world ruler, will be defeated and Israel will be saved. This will be discussed later in this book. Therefore, it is logical to look for a similar end time event associated with these two eclipses. I knew from past study that God was going to take vengeance on the Arab Muslims in the near future (see arguments below). This seems to be confirmed by the Jewish Sabbath reading for the respective Sabbaths on which the total eclipses take place.

I have reached conclusions on all six lunar eclipses through this pattern of analysis. It is as if God is giving us a heavenly sign and telling us to check the Sabbath reading for coming events.

Sabbath readings for the first two are as follows:

The Fast of Esther - Saturday March 3, 2007.

Israel sees the need to worship and seek God.

Sabbath reading: Exodus 27:20–30:10, Reading on Temple worship.

Deuteronomy 25:17–19, God's promise to blot out memory of Amalekites.

I Samuel 15:2–34 – Punishment of Amalek (Edomites descendents of Esau) the forefather of the Arab nations. Esther 3:13- Note: this is the day of the decree written to kill all Jews.

Shushan Purim - Saturday February 21, 2008, (Sabbatical year 5768).

God to take vengeance on the Arab Muslims. War with in the year?

Sabbath reading: Exodus 30:11–34 to, and 35,

Judgment against house of Esau.

Prophets: I Kings 18:1–39, Elijah's victory over Baal at Mt. Carmel.

WAR BEFORE THE RAPTURE

I believe these first two eclipses have application to Israel's next major war. For my arguments I go again to similitude's (to compare, by implication, to resemble, liken, consider) found in the book of Numbers. Again let me remind you in the life story of Joshua there is a complete similitude of those called by Jesus from his coming to earth to his second coming to earth. I consider every event in Joshua a prophetic similitude.

During the forty years of the wilderness wandering Israel had five major conflicts; four of these similitudes have been completed, with the last soon to take place (see references below).

The **first** was the Jewish revolt which culminated in the destruction of the Temple in AD 70 (Similitude, Numbers 14:45).

Second was the 1948 war when Israel became a nation. (Read Similitude, Numbers 21:1–3)

The 1967 war was **number three** and used by God as the Fifth Seal of Revelation. This was unique because it was 1900 years since the Jews had control of the old city, and were able to approach the Temple Mount (Read Similitude, Numbers 21:24-25). As already mentioned the exact day the Temple Mount was taken could be calculated by data from the bible.

The **Fourth** war was the 1973 Yom Kippur war (Read Similitude, Numbers 21:33–35).

The similitude, for the **fifth** war is found in Numbers 31:11. This will be the final war, before the rapture, and will result in total victory over the Palestinians and their descendants. In this Fifth similitude it says:

> Then the LORD spoke to Moses, saying, "Take full vengeance for the sons of Israel on the Midianites; afterward you will be gathered to your people." Moses spoke to the people, saying, "Arm men from among you for the war, that they may go against Midian to execute the LORD'S vengeance on Midian. A thousand from each tribe of all the tribes of Israel you shall send to the war." So there were furnished from the thousands of Israel, a thousand from each tribe, twelve thousand armed for war. Moses sent them, a thousand from each tribe, to the war, and Phinehas the son of Eleazar the priest, to the war with them, and the holy vessels and the trumpets for the alarm in his hand. So they made war against Midian, just as the LORD had commanded Moses, and they killed every male. They killed the kings of Midian along with the rest of their slain: Evi and Rekem and Zur and Hur and Reba, the five kings of Midian; they also killed Balaam the son of Beor with the sword. The sons of Israel captured the women of Midian and their little ones; and all their cattle and all their flocks and all their goods they plundered. Then they burned all their cities where they lived and all their camps with fire. They took all the spoil and all the prey, both of man and of beast (Numbers 31:1–11).

At God's request Israel will take holy vengeance on the Arab Muslims (the worshipers of the crescent moon) that have been troubling Israel for many years. Many of their leaders will be killed such as, Hassan Narallah, Khaled Mash'al, Mahmoud Abbas, and Bashar Assad. Along with the king of Mesopotamia; towns will be plundered and burned.

Other scriptures that apply to this war are:

> But on Mount Zion there will be those who escape, and it will be holy. And the house of Jacob will possess their possessions.

> Then the house of Jacob will be a fire and the house of Joseph a flame; but the house of Esau will be as stubble. And they will set them on fire and consume them, so that there will be no survivor of the house of Esau, "For the LORD has spoken. (Obadiah 1:17–18).

The temple mount will be reclaimed but not built on at this time. As in the past, Ephraim and Manasseh will team up to fight against the descendants of Esau, which include the Palestinians; but this time it will be side by side with Israel and the victory will be like a brush fire.

> The burden of Damascus. Behold, Damascus is taken away from being a city, and it shall be a ruinous heap. The cities of Aroer are forsaken: they shall be for flocks, which shall lie down, and none shall make them afraid. The fortress also shall cease from Ephraim, and the kingdom from Damascus, and the remnant of Syria: they shall be as the glory of the children of Israel, saith the LORD of hosts: (Isaiah 17:1–3 KJV).

Damascus will be totally destroyed. In my own thought I imaged Syria would launch WMD (weapons of mass destruction) chemicals and the wind would blow it back on Damascus and destroy it that way. However, even if the WMD start the war, it sounds like the retaliation may be the new mega bombs and conventional weapons. This war will continue south into Jordan (cities of Aroer). One cannot rule out this coming war being similar to the six day war, but even more decisive.

"The fortress shall cease from Ephraim (Isaiah 17:3), this could mean the West Bank is free from the enemy. Or it may be saying Ephraim has participated in their last battle of reclaiming the land for Israel, as this dispensation is drawing to a close. In fact Ephraim may receive this strip of land, during the millennial reign that includes Damascus (Ezekiel 47:13–48:35). Wouldn't that be poetic justice?

Damascus and Syria will not be considered a power during the tribulation or the coming Magog war. Syria will be a glory to Israel when they lay claim to this land.

> Thus says the LORD, "For three transgressions of Damascus and for four I will not revoke its punishment, because they threshed Gilead with implements of sharp iron." 'So I will send fire upon the house of Hazael and it will consume the citadels of Ben-hadad.' 'I will also break the gate bar of Damascus, and cut off the inhabitant from the valley of Aven, and him who holds the scepter, from Beth-eden; so the people of Aram will go exiled to Kir,' Says the LORD. Thus says the LORD, "For three transgressions of Gaza and for four I will not revoke its punishment, because they deported an entire population to deliver it up to Edom." 'So I will send fire upon the wall of Gaza and it will consume her citadels.' 'I will also cut off the inhabitant from Ashdod, and him who holds the scepter, from Ashkelon; I will even unleash my power upon Ekron, and the remnant of the Philistines will perish,' 'Says the Lord GOD. Thus says the LORD,' "For three transgressions of Tyre and for four I will not revoke its punishment, because they delivered up an entire population to Edom and did not remember the covenant of brotherhood. (Amos 1:3–9).
>
> Moreover, what are you to Me, O Tyre, Sidon and all the regions of Philistia? Are you rendering me recompense? But if you do recompense me, swiftly and speedily I will return your recompense on your head. (Joel 3:4).

I anticipate Middle East events to grow in intensity starting around the total lunar eclipses of March 3, 2008. Troubles and provocations will increase and war will probably break out with in the year. A coalition of nations will fight a major war against the terrorists such as the Hezbollah, Fattah, Hamas, Islamic Jihad and Al-Qaida. It does not appear Iran will be directly involved, but this war will be a major defeat because Iran directs and supplies most of the equipment and chaos. Rather it appears the war will be centered in Lebanon, Syria, West Bank and Gaza. This alliance of nations with Israel will be led by the brothers Ephraim (Britain) and Manasseh (America). This will be the first Middle East war where the brothers of Jacob fight side by side with Joseph (Jews). But in reality it will be God's vengeance on Islamic Arab nations (similitude, Numbers 3:1–6). Damascus will be destroyed and the Islamic religion will suffer the world over, and there may be some kind of drought or pestilence on them as well.

One thing is certain: If the interpretation of these signs is correct, and this war is the vengeance of God (I believe it is), His print will be on it and it will be more spectacular than the six day war. What a fitting climax for the church and Israel -- witnessing the last war in Israel before the rapture. There will certainly be rejoicing in the streets. I would sure like to be there during the Feast of Tabernacles.

As a positive result of this war, Israel will prosper and will likely become a member of the EU. Peace and prosperity will temporarily prevail in Israel. The walls being built in Israel will come down. Lebanon will become a Christian nation again, and Christianity will flourish around the world. Once we understand the overview of God's plan, where we are in the Seals, and what will take place after the rapture, we can concentrate on current signs and the soon return of our Lord.

Jesus required the Jewish nation to expect and watch for His first advent; and the Church needs to be in a position to bring many souls into the kingdom without fearing the rapture.

SIGNS IN THE STARS

A third sign of the heavens Jesus tells us to watch for are signs in the stars. In the (Luke 21:25) He uses the Greek word "Astron (G798). I believe He is referring to Asteroids and/or Meteorites. Just as with solar flares and moon eclipses, one can get on line and monitor the NEO (near earth objects).xiii

To date there are 4,406 close approaches being monitored, of which 833 are known PHAs (Potentially Hazardous Asteroids). It is the ones not known that are of more concern. When it was believed that the (433) Eros asteroid was on a collision course with earth a space probe "NEAR was launched on February 17, 1996 and actually landed on this 20 x 8 mile rock on February 12, 2001.xiv When will there be an event on earth? Note: There is an Asteroid belt orbiting the Sun, and on October 1991 asteroid 951 Gaspra was visited by the Galileo spacecraft and became the first asteroid to have hi-resolution images taken of it. xv

Summing up these signs in the heavens, the largest solar flare on the **sun** ever recorded occurred on 4 November 2003. The first total eclipse of the **moon** was be in the longitude of Israel and was on the fast of Esther, March 3, 2007. This eclipse was unique in that it is partly visible from every continent around the world.

The first moon landing on the moon was July 20, 1969.xvi A sign in the stars the space probe "NEAR was launched February 17, 1996, landed on asteroid Eros February 12, 2001.

These observations serve only as a sampling of signs in the heavens that are available. Now one can see how Jesus was teaching us what could happen when the "Heavenly Sign of the Sixth Seal is opened. It may be a whopping solar flare along with the dislodging of meteoroids. When they are detected coming toward earth men's hearts will fail for the coming terror. As these stars strike the earth it will cause extensive damage; earth quakes will rattle human-kind and, dust will be tossed in the air. **The sun will be as sack cloth, the moon will be as blood**, and three days later there will be a total lunar eclipse.

As believers we will be safe from this destruction, just as Rahab's house was safe-guarded when the walls fell and they were set outside the camp (Similitude, Joshua 6). There were seven trumpet blasts and a shout that brought the walls of Jericho down. However, we are told the seven trumpets of wrath will not be allowed to blow until the church is set outside the camp (raptured) (Revelation: 7), but there will be a shout (1Thessilonians 4:16).

We have laid out the road map as far as the last sign before the rapture. The next exit is where we want to get off. If we miss that exit there will be many more signs, but there will be no safe exit out of the tribulation for most believers. (Note that those Persian Magi familiar with the prophet Daniel's prophesies could discern (or at least find confirmation) from the stars that Messiah had been born. How much more observant should we be of the heavenly signs?

ANOTHER VIEW OF SOLAR AND LUNAR ECLIPSES

The following is the interview part of an article by J. R. Church (Prophecy in the News). [xvii] It is a summation of two TV interviews by Church and his associate, Gary Stearman, with Pastor Mark Biltz, El Shaddai Ministries in Bonny Lake, Washington. [xviii]

I was so pleased to find someone investigating the heavenly signs, as Jesus commanded, and even more encouraged finding a TV ministry willing to air these findings. Over the years I have sent copies of this synopsis to several well known ministries and received no response other than a turn down. When one analyzes the fear of receiving this teaching, it is apparent that the existence of just one unfulfilled sign can kill two sacred cows in the main-stream premillennial camp. First it proves that there will be another sign take place before the rapture. Thereby negating the common teaching there will be no more signs before the return of the Lord, and He could return at any moment. Second it destroys the theory of imminent return because it demonstrates God will not violate his character by failing to warn of His impending wrath. Nor will God fail to share His plan with his called out. I believe the theory of imminent return has restrained Christians from teaching and understanding the true plan God has laid out. I am convinced the church (those in the light) will not be walking in darkness when Christ comes for his bride. I thank God I can share some of brother Blitz's work with you.

Solar and Lunar Eclipses in 2014/15

by J. R. Church

As you may know, this year is a Sabbatical Year in the Jewish calendar. Starting next September 29, 2008, a new Sabbatical cycle will commence. It will run for seven years and conclude with another Sabbatical Year in 2014/15.

Also, you may know that Daniel's seventieth week will be a seven-year Sabbatical cycle. Students of biblical prophecy have long compared Daniel's seventieth week with the Tribulation Period as laid out in the book of Revelation.

Intrigued with the Scriptures that repeat over and over again that our Savior's Second Coming will be heralded with signs in the heavens, in which the sun will be turned into darkness and the moon into blood, Pastor Mark Biltz went on the Internet, to a U.S. Government web site, to see if he could find any solar or lunar eclipses over the next few years that might be significant.

To his surprise, he found four lunar eclipses and two solar eclipses in the Sabbatical Year of 2014 and 2015. Also, he noticed that they all appear on Jewish Holy Days!

Lunar Eclipses

The four lunar eclipses will occur on:

> Passover, April 15, 2014
> Feast of Tabernacles, October 8, 2014
> Passover, April 4, 2015 and
> Feast of Tabernacles, September 28, 2015

This is most unusual. It is a rare occurrence for four lunar cycles to happen on successive Passover and the Feast of Tabernacles (*Sukkot*) observances. It will not happen again for hundreds of years. However, Mark found that a series of four lunar eclipses on these particular holy days did occur in the twentieth century -- not once, but twice! The first set occurred in 1949-1950, the year after Israel became a state! The second set happened in 1967-1968, the year Israel liberated Jerusalem! Such a phenomenon is nigh unto impossible, unless it was set up by Divine design. Mark looked back in history and noticed that the last time this set of four lunar eclipses occurred on Passover and *Sukkot* was in 1493, the year after Columbus sailed the ocean blue and Spain expelled all Jews.

Mark is convinced that God was telling the beleaguered Jews that He was fully aware of their circumstances! In that case, we wonder what is God telling the Jews in the 1949 and 1967 lunar eclipses? And, as we look at the next seven years, we wonder, "What is God telling Israel through the upcoming lunar eclipses? Is it possible that these are fulfilling biblical prophecies?

Solar Eclipses

In addition to the four lunar eclipses in 2014-15, Mark also found two solar eclipses. They will occur on:

Adar 29/Nisan 1, March 20, 2015
The Feast of Trumpets, September 13, 2015

These two dates are quite significant because they are special days in the Jewish calendar. For example, it was on *Nisan* 1, the first anniversary of the Exodus, that Moses raised up the tabernacle for the first time and the glory of God descended. Two weeks later, the Chosen People observed their first Pentecost since the Exodus.

Nisan 1 marks the beginning of the religious festival cycle. Six months later, on Tishri 1, the Jews observe Rosh Hashanah, the Feast of Trumpets. This day is highly prophetic, because it is said to be the anniversary of the Creation of Adam. It is Adam's birthday. And, even though it is a Jewish observance, it is prophetically significant as a day for Gentile nations.

It is the day when God will sit down upon His throne of Judgment and take the books in his hand. That is when He will begin the judgment of the world. So, a solar eclipse on Rosh Hashanah could precede the Second Coming of Christ in power and great glory, and fulfill the biblical description.

The Solar Eclipse This Year

Coming up this summer, there will be the first of three solar eclipses on the day that introduces the first of *Av* (August 1, 2008). That's right, all three solar eclipses will be on the biblical date of *Av* 1, for the next three years -- 2008, 2009, and 2010. Our Gregorian calendar dates are:

> ***Av* 1 - August 1, 2008 - partial eclipse**
> ***Av* 1 - July 22, 2009 - partial eclipse**
> ***Av* 1 - July 11, 2010 - partial eclipse**

In the Jewish calendar, they are all on the first of *Av*, the day when Jews lament the destruction of their temples. As the story goes, Moses caught the people worshiping the Golden Calf on *Tammuz* 17. Therefore, the three weeks from *Tammuz* 17 to *Av* 9 are called "the dark time and "between the straits. It is the most sorrowful time of the year for Jews. From *Av* 1-9, no bathing is allowed; no comforts; no clean clothes; the Jew takes his shoes off; sits on an overturned chair and reads the book of Lamentations.

However, there will come a time when God will reverse the fast days and turn them into feast days. Zechariah said:

Thus saith the LORD of hosts; The fast of the fourth month [Tammuz 17], and the fast of the fifth [Av 9], and the fast of the seventh, and the fast of the tenth, shall be to the house of Judah joy and gladness, and cheerful feasts; therefore love the truth and peace (Zech. 8:19).

Mark Biltz seems to think that the solar eclipses on *Av* 1 could change the course of history, because solar eclipses are designed for Gentile nations, whereas lunar eclipses are designed for Israel. Therefore, he thinks that God could begin judging the nations this summer. Will there be a war in Israel this summer? It is entirely possible. If so, then the solar eclipse could be announcing judgment upon the world -- a sobering thought!

In the above article Mark Biltz articulated the same conclusions I have about the heavenly signs. There will be a war this year, and these signs point to the 7 years of tribulation.

I take these heavenly signs seriously and try to apply them to specific events just as I have other signs in the bible. These events may have different applications than I assign to them, and they will certainly have more points to ponder than conveyed in this article. There are many ways to study these signs for more and deeper meanings. Again I suggest studying the Sabbatical weekly readings associated with each sign (eclipse).

Other examples: when one goes to the government website we find 2 solar eclipses in 1901. The first is a total eclipses on May 18, when 120 years is added to this date you come to May 17, 2021 (Sivan 6) the possible date of the sea of glass rapture (Revelation 15). Or, we could take the partial eclipses of November 11th, add 120 years and come to November 10th (the 28th of Cheshvan) a possible date for the sheep and goats judgment of Matthew 25.

As for the sabbatical cycle, there are different beliefs. Some writers suggest the cycle is a year later, while others believe it starts on Nisan 1, others on Tishri 1, and still others teach it starts on Tishri 22.

It is clear we have a lot to study and learn but when writing an end time synopsis one must stop somewhere. We all will be learning when the Lord comes.

THE RAPTURE

Luke 21:28 tells us to look up when we see these signs begin to happen because our redemption is drawing near, and we are to pray that we can be found worthy to escape those things that are coming (tribulation). But in the parallel passage in (Revelation 6) everyone will be able to recognize when the wrath of the Lamb has come. For some there will be redemption, for others wrath.

Jesus then opens the **seventh and last seal** (Revelation 8:1, Luke 21:28) thus completing the work He was found worthy to do. This last seal reveals seven trumpets that tell us what will take place in the following seven years. In a nut shell these trumpets will reveal the **"Wrath of the Lamb, "Wrath of Satan, and Wrath of Man** and out of the Seventh trumpet the **"Wrath of God.**

> Then the seventh angel sounded; and there were loud voices in heaven, saying, "The kingdom of the world has become the kingdom of our Lord and of His Christ; and He will reign forever and ever." (Revelation 11:15).

These seven trumpets were not allowed to sound **"until we have sealed the servants of our God on their foreheads.** This will be done during the transition period between dispensations we reviewed above.

It is during this period that the 144,000 Israelites receive new bodies being "first fruits (Revelation 14:4). Unlike the raptured church, they remain on earth during the tribulation trying to convince others to take the mark of God, on their foreheads even though it may cost them their lives. I believe many of the 144,000 know who they are now.

I pray that during this transition period we will be able to bring others into the kingdom. Just as those found in Rahab's house were saved and set outside the camp of Israel (Similitude, Joshua 6:23) so will the church be saved from the wrath to come and be transported to heaven and receive their new bodies.

> And not only this, but also we ourselves, having the first fruits of the Spirit, even we ourselves groan within ourselves, waiting eagerly for our adoption as sons, the redemption of our body. (Romans 8:23).

> Behold, I tell you a mystery; we will not all sleep, but we will all be changed, in a moment, in the twinkling of an eye, at the last trumpet; for the trumpet will sound, and the dead will be raised imperishable, and we will be changed. (1 Corinthians 15:51-52).

> But we do not want you to be uninformed, brethren, about those who are asleep, so that you will not grieve as do the rest who have no hope. For if we believe that Jesus died and rose again, even so God will bring with Him those who have fallen asleep in Jesus. For this we say to you by the word of the Lord, that we, who are alive and remain until the coming of the Lord, will not precede those who have fallen asleep. For the Lord Himself will descend from heaven with a shout, with the voice of the archangel and with the trumpet of God, and the dead in Christ will rise first. Then we who are alive and remain will be caught up together with them in the clouds to meet the Lord in the air, and so we shall always be with the Lord. Therefore comfort one another with these words. (1 Thessalonians 4:13–18).

God true to his character will send a warning sign before the rapture. Think of all the various ways God warned his people in the past, by a prophet laying on his side several days, or walking through the street naked, or by angels, or plagues or heavenly signs.

I am convinced, regardless of the year the rapture takes place, that there will be a heavenly sign on the tenth of Nisan which everyone will see: This will serve as an announcement (RSVP) that the wedding will take place (in less than 60 days), on Pentecost. If this scenario is correct, we can expect that on April 10, 2014, there will be a great earthquake, the sun will turn black and the moon will become like blood. We know that on Passover, April 15, 2014, there will be total lunar eclipses, all these heavenly signs warn of a coming dispensational change culminating on Sunday, June 8, 2014, with rapture (new bodies) of the followers of Jesus the Christ, both dead and living!

> After these things I looked, and behold, a great multitude which no one could count, from every nation and all tribes and peoples and tongues, standing before the throne and before the Lamb, clothed in white robes, and palm branches were in their hands; (Revelation 7:9).

> Then one of the elders answered, saying to me, 'These who are clothed in the white robes, who are they, and where have they come from?' I said to him, 'My lord, you know.' And he said to me, "These are the ones who come out of the great tribulation, and they have washed their robes and made them white in the blood of the Lamb". (Revelation 7:13-14).

> And he said to me, "These are they which came out of great tribulation, and have washed their robes, and made them white in the blood of the Lamb." (Revelation 7:14, KJV [Ref. Revelation 1:9].

EXPLANATIONS OF TERMS

Before we continue with the time line I want to give you <u>my understanding of terms</u> we will encounter in the rest of this study. Terms like beasts, ten toes (kings), antichrist, Shiite, Sunni, and Mystery Babylon. Etc.

The area of God's prophetic word we are about to study will teach us about world governments both past and future. But more importantly it will show us that powerful, supernatural spiritual rulers are attached to those kingdoms. Therefore, I believe we should not necessarily consider these empires as the largest or greatest nations of their respective periods of time; rather we look on them as the path Satan used to spread his seed and the spiritual principalities he uses to accomplish it.

In Daniel chapter 2 four historic world kingdoms are likened to a statue. The **Babylon Empire** represents the head of gold; the next empire was **Medo-Persia**, the chest and arms of silver; the **Grecian** the belly and thighs composed of Bronze. The forth empire had "**legs of iron, its feet partly iron and partly** of clay (verse 33), representing the **Roman Empire** and its successors from the time of Christ to the present.

In Daniel seven the spiritual analogy is placed on the four empires as they were likened unto beasts. The first is like a **lion** (verse 4), next like a **bear** (verse 5), then a **leopard** with four wings and four heads (verse 6), and the present beast the deteriorating Roman Empire "fourth beast dreadful and, exceedingly strong and it had large iron teeth (verse 7). This Roman Beast also had **"ten horns and another horn came up and made war against the saints."** (Revelation 13:7). This horn alludes to a coming beast (the Seventh) which **we will find rising to power during the great tribulation. (Daniel 7:20–21).**

In Daniel eight we find the Medo-Persia and Grecian Empires will be identified as a ram and a goat in latter days. This tells us where the last two (number 7 and 8) world empires will come from and aids in identifying the spiritual power over them.

> Behold, I am going to let you know what will occur at the final period of the indignation, for it pertains to the appointed time of the end. 'The ram which you saw with the two horns represents the kings of Media and Persia.' 'The shaggy goat represents the kingdom of Greece, and the large horn that is between his eyes is the first king.' The broken horn and the four horns that arose in its place represent four kingdoms which will arise from his nation, although not with his power." (Daniel 8:19–22).

All the Beasts of Daniel and Revelation are from the Middle East, and they all identify with the, spiritual wickedness of crescent moon worship (Islam). The Middle East is today just as Daniel said it would be at this time in history. The feet would be -- like iron mixed with clay, both weak and strong, and unable to stick together. Like democracy and Islam, like Muslim and Communist, like Jew and Muslim, like Christ and Mohammad, like Christian and Islam, or Shiite and Sunnis. God has always tried to teach us that we are in a spiritual battle:

> For our struggle is not against flesh and blood, but against the rulers, against the powers, against the world forces of this darkness, against the spiritual forces of wickedness in the heavenly places. (Ephesians 6:12).

This truth is summed up:

Little children, make sure no one deceives you; the one who practices righteousness is righteous, just as He is righteous; the one who practices sin is of the devil; for the devil has sinned from the beginning. The Son of God appeared for this purpose, to destroy the works of the devil. No one who is born of God practices sin, because His seed abides in him; and he cannot sin, because he is born of God. By this the children of God and the children of the devil are obvious: anyone who does not practice righteousness is not of God, nor the one who does not love his brother. For this is the message which you have heard from the beginning, that we should love one another; not as Cain, who was of the evil one and slew his brother. And for what reason did he slay him? Because his deeds were evil, and his brother's were righteous. (1 John 3:7–12).

We see from the above passages that seed will produce its own kind. God has always desired to keep His seed (Jesus the Christ is the word of God) pure and not mingled with the seed of Satan (the word of the serpent). God said: I will put enmity between you (Satan) and the woman, And between your seed and her seed; (Genesis 3:15).

Satan is the source of the evil seed, and is behind these powers of darkness.

You are of your father the devil, and you want to do the desires of your father. He was a murderer from the beginning, and does not stand in the truth because there is no truth in him. Whenever he speaks a lie, he speaks from his own nature, for he is a liar and the father of lies. (John 8:44).

With this background we can move to Revelation 13 and 17, and identify the final two beasts that are yet to come, along with their spiritual leaders.

THE BEAST WITH SEVEN HEADS

Revelation 17:10 introduces a beast with seven heads, which is likened to seven empires both past and future. They are: Egypt, Assyria, Babylon, Medo-Persia, Greece, Rome (the present empire since Christ) and the seventh is still to arise, and will come for a "short time. Then last, the eighth beast is identified as "one that was and is not. These seven heads are also known as seven mountains and seven Kings. These eight beasts are all identified with having blasphemous names on their heads and have a satanic prince or king as their leader. The definition of "blasphemy from Strong's -- G989; vilification (especially against God):—blasphemy, evil speaking, railing (Revelation 13:1). This means they all speak evil of God. I believe not only do these empires rail against God but the evil spirits produce an opposite spirit of God. Back through the years and in the future this was accomplished via the worship of the moon. This moon worship has come down through the Muslim religion for hundreds of years. This religion is anti God in its writings, its actions and its own prophecies. It teaches its worshippers to kill their enemies, not love them. It teaches taking a kingdom by force, not by the word of God. It denies the deity of Christ. It is a system of works without grace. This list goes on and on, reversing God's truth by calling evil good and good evil.

Following are some examples of the seed of Satan via his writings of the Qur'ran, which bears fruit after its own kind.

> O Muslim! There is a Jew hiding behind me, so kill him.... We have put enmity and hatred amongst them till the Day of Resurrection. (Sura 5:60.64).

> Allah begets not and was not begotten, that is, he is no Son: and no one is like him, which means he is no Holy Spirit. (Sura 112).

> Believers (Muslims), take neither Jews nor Christians to be your friends: they are friends with one another. Whoever of you seeks their friendship shall become one of their number, and God does not guide (those Jewish and Christian) wrong-doers. *(Sura 5:51)*.

The Bible is unique among the world's religious writings, as it reveals the word of God and prophecies the beginning from the end. The Bible declares: "Who is the liar but the one who denies that Jesus is the Christ? This is the antichrist, the one who denies the Father and the Son." (1 John 2:22).

TEN KINGS

The vision in Daniel 2 shows the Roman Empire dividing into two iron legs, Eastern and Western and then into feet of iron and clay and finally toes of iron and clay. These **ten toes** are likened into ten horns in Daniel 7, where another little horn comes up among them. These ten horns (which have ten crowns) are also ten kings. They are present today, but never receive empire recognition. They will be subordinate to the antichrist but will receive power via the eighth kingdom. (Revelation 17:12). Five of these from the Eastern leg may include Syria, Lebanon, Jordan, Saudi Arabia., and Iraq all out of the Middle East. You may have noticed that Turkey and Iran are excluded from this list, because areas of Turkey and Iran will be part of the western toes that will come out of the (Ezekiel 38–39), Medo-Persian war (Russia-Iran).

Similar to the Babylonian "Lion, The Persian "Bear, and the Grecian "Leopard, the next beast to appear in Revelation is described as "resembling a leopard. (Revelation 13:2). I believe the "little horn mentioned above will be the next world beast described in Revelation 13:1-7. He looks like a leopard indicating his Greek heritage via general Seleucus King of Syria. This Beast (the seventh, the antichrist) will rise to power the last three and one half years of the tribulation. The true spiritual leader of this empire is Satan himself, having taken a human body (Revelation 13:2). However, we must remember the empire of this seventh beast is restricted to 1260 days even though he makes a covenant with Israel at the start of the seven years of tribulation.

I found it rather difficult to identify who the feet of iron and clay represent until I identified the last two beasts. It then becomes obvious we are presently in a transition stage where one fourth the earth is dominated by the evil seed of Islam religion.

Present Day / Summary

The world has been under the influence of the iron legs of the Roman Empire since before Christ. This fourth beast of Daniel (the sixth empire) was described as follows:

> Then I desired to know the exact meaning of the fourth beast, which was *different* from all the others, exceedingly dreadful, with its teeth of iron and its claws of bronze, and which devoured, crushed and trampled down the remainder with its feet, (Daniel 7:19)

We have covered in some detail God's 120 year end time plan, and Christ is the beginning and end of every phase. As the plan started Christ gathered his forces in the first seal, in preparation to keep the promises of God to redeem the Church "the bride of Christ, and Israel "the wife of God along with the Promised Land.

When the Second Seal was opened the forces of good went against this iron toothed beast that was taking peace from the earth via WWI. As a result of this war the forces of good gave this iron beast a thorough thrashing. More specifically the Ottoman Empire, which I believe was the eastern leg of the Roman Empire (which was already Muslim) was destroyed, thereby preparing the land for Israel. I believe this is where the Eastern leg of the Roman Empire became the mixed feet of iron and clay which has developed into the Middle East countries as we know them today. The eastern leg of the Roman Empire became iron and clay sooner than the western leg. The western leg digressed to iron and clay (Muslim) after WWII.

The Third Seal brought famine and caused people to relocate and started the return of Jewish people to Israel.

The Fourth Seal brought WWII, and prepared the Jewish people for the Promised Land. This seal is still with us today as we are progressing down the list of birth pangs described in this seal. This war brought an end to the western iron leg of the Roman Empire as it has also deteriorated into a foot of iron mixed with clay. I believe countries making up this western foot are identified in Ezekiel 38 with Gog as their leader. Remember how WWII reached down into North Africa, and how Iran and Persia will be associated with those countries.

In the end this iron toothed beast that has carried the evil seed all these years has come home to roost in the Middle East among the worshipers of the moon god.

We must also recall how the two spiritual beings were given power over one fourth the earth to carry out some of the birth pangs of the Fourth Seal, our present day situation. Let me remind you these two spiritual beings are not given a kingdom or an empire until after the toes are formed; therefore the feet of iron and clay are still considered the deteriorating Roman Empire. The seventh empire of the antichrist will come from the five toes of the left foot and the eighth empire will come from the toes of the right foot.

It is my belief the five toes of the eastern foot will start forming after the defeat of Syria and Palestine which we discussed earlier in this book. The five toes of the western foot will form only after the defeat of Gog and his followers shortly after the rapture of the church. We will learn later that defeat is the Ezekiel 38–38 war of the first three trumpet of the wrath of the Lamb.

ANTICHRIST

The antichrist will be an eleventh toe (horn) out of the ten toes. He will be known as a peace maker after the Magog war that takes place near the first part of the seven years of tribulation. His empire will start in the middle and last exactly 1260 days. Some of the identifying marks of the antichrist found in the Bible are:

The King of Babylon (Isaiah 14:4).

Ruler of Tyre (Ezekiel 28:2).

Stern-Faced King (Daniel 8:23).

The Little Horn (Daniel 7:8).

The Prince that Shall Come (Daniel 9:26).

The Assyrian (Isaiah 10:24).

The Antichrist (1 John 2:18).

The First Beast (Revelation 11:7, Revelation 13:1).

In his book "Unveiling the Man of Sin Dr. Joe Van Koevering presents convincing proofs as to where the Antichrist might come from, and whom he might be. On page112 of his book, Dr. Van Koevering puts forth as a candidate Prince Hassan bin Talal of Jordan. He is an uncle to the current king of Jordan, a Sunni of the Hashemite line which have authority over the Temple Mount xix
According to the London-based Palestinian daily Al-Quds Al-Arabi, Israel has come to an understanding with Palestinian Authority leader Mahmoud Abbas to transfer custody of the Temple Mount to Jordan and to allow 90,000 Arab residents of east Jerusalem to receive Jordanian citizenship. The unofficial draft deal, made in the light of the November 2007 US sponsored Middle East Peace Summit, seeks to acknowledge Jordan's historic role as custodian Jerusalem's Muslim Holy Sites and build on principles established in the 1994 peace accord. Furthermore, there is discussion to trade control of Arab neighborhoods in Jerusalem in return for larger Israeli settlement blocs on the West Bank. "The most important thing is to preserve the Jewish and democratic state of Israel," said Vice Premier Haim Ramon in a Monday interview with Israel Radio. As of this writing, this Prime Minister's office has denied that any official agreement has been reached.

I still believe it will take a major defeat of the Sunnis before the wall around Jerusalem will be torn down. But it is obvious the ground work is under way to enable the sharing of the Temple Mount by Jews, Christians and Muslims. The sharing of the Temple Mount will be the obvious manifestation of the "Woman who rides the Beast.

> And the ten horns which you saw, and the beast, these will hate the harlot and will make her desolate and naked, and will eat her flesh and will burn her up with fire. (Revelation 17:16).

Any time the seed of God mingles (goes whoring) with the seed of Satan, there results a union that is displeasing to God. So it is very important that the Christians and the Jews not participate in Satan's ways or his lies. I believe the future antichrist is leading this effort even today.

THE EIGHTH BEAST

This eighth beast has two horns like a lamb, and he "once was and is to come. (Revelation 17:11). I believe the two horns identify him with the past Medo-Persian Empire (today's Russia and Iran).

> Behold, I am going to let you know what will occur at the final period of the indignation, for it pertains to the appointed time of the end. The ram which you saw with the two horns represents the kings of Media and Persia. (Daniel 8:19).

This eighth and last beast will help the antichrist during the first part of his 1260 day rule. But according to Revelation 9:15. He will go to war against the antichrist during the last 391 days (an hour and day and month and year).(Revelation9:15).

The eighth beast "The beast which was and is not, is himself also an eighth and is one of the seven, and he goes to destruction. (Revelation 17:11).

The identity of this eighth beast comes from one of the past seven; he had two horns and came out of the bottomless pit or the Abyss during the fifth trumpet. (Revelation 17:8, Revelation 9:11). I believe this corresponds with the Medo-Persia-type Empire. The spiritual leader's name is Abaddon or Gog. Therefore, I believe Gog was the controlling evil spirit of the Medo- Persian Empire during Daniel's day.

> Then he said, "Do you understand why I came to you? But I shall now return to fight against the prince of Persia; so I am going forth, and behold, the prince of Greece is about to come. (Daniel 10:20).

I see the events in (Daniel 10–12), as a duel prophecy fulfilled before Christ's return and thus, in these "latter days (Daniel 11:14), we are dealing again with the spiritual leader Gog and a rising Medo-Persian Empire in today's world known as Russia and Iran. (See

Ezekiel 38). At the same time we have a Grecian type empire forming in the Middle East (being lead by Satan) out of which the Antichrist will emerge.

GOG THE SPIRIT KING

> For our struggle is not against flesh and blood, but against the rulers, against the powers, against the world forces of this darkness, against the spiritual forces of wickedness in the heavenly places. (Ephesians 6:12).

> Then I saw three evil spirits that looked like frogs; they came out of the mouth of the dragon, out of the mouth of the beast and out of the mouth of the false prophet. They are spirits of demons performing miraculous signs, and they go out to the kings of the whole world, to gather them for the battle on the great day of God Almighty. (Revelation 16:13–14).

> Thus the Lord showed me, and behold a swarm of locusts were coming, and, behold, one of the young devastating locusts was Gog, the King. (Amos 7:1, Septuagint Translation).

> Son of man, set your face toward Gog of the land of Magog, the prince of Rosh, Meshech and Tubal, and prophesy against him. (Ezekiel 38:2).

> Sharpen the arrows, fill the quivers! The LORD has aroused the spirit of the kings of the Medes, because His purpose is against Babylon to destroy it; For it is the vengeance of the LORD, vengeance for His temple. (Jeremiah 51:11).

Gog is then an evil spirit who is exercises authority over other evil spirits. He is a spiritual ruler over the Medo-Persian Empire, the chief prince of the land of Magog.

In my opinion Gog was initially defeated and imprisoned by the angel Michael (Daniel 10-13). I believe he was recently released from the pit when the fourth trumpet sounded and a spirit rider of the pale horse called "Death came on the world scene. This was around 1935 when WWII started, which eventually led to the "Holocaust. At that time in history, Persia elected to side with Hitler so they changed their name to Iran, because they wanted to be identified with the Arian race instead of the Arabs.

This means that Gog is still active today, and will marshal his forces against Israel again. We know Gog's next defeat will be the (Ezekiel 38-39) nuclear war that takes place right after the rapture. This Medo-Persian (Russia-Iran) alliance is obviously forming this very day. This nuclear war will be the first three trumpets of the tribulation. (See Chart A)

As prophesied, Gog and his forces will be soundly defeated, and Gog will find himself in the pit again. About three years later in the middle of the tribulation when the fifth trumpet sounds (Revelation 9:1–11). Gog will again be released from the bottomless pit.

> They have tails like scorpions, and stings; and in their tails is their power to hurt men for five months. They have as king over them, the angel of the abyss; his name in Hebrew is Abaddon, and in the Greek he has the name Apollyon. (Revelation 9:10–11), Abaddon, means, destroyer, ruin, perdition

After his release Gog will help the antichrist for a while, and then strike out on his own; ultimately becoming the eighth beast and last world ruler.

In the end Gog and the ten kings are defeated (along with the nations) by the personal coming of the Lord Jesus (Revelation 16:12–16). Gog is finally cast into the lake of fire (Revelation19:20).

Spiritual Gog may be involved again at the end of the thousand year reign: "and will come out to deceive the nations which are in the four corners of the earth, Gog and Magog, to gather them together for the war; the number of them is like the sand of the seashore." (Revelation 20:8).

Remember I described the book of Esther as a similitude about Gog. The ruling kings in the days of Esther had a title of "Agag which is believed to refer to Gog. "**Their king** (Israel's) **will be greater than Agag;** (Numbers 24:7). See Strong's (H90) of uncertain derivation (compare H89); flame; Agag, a title of Amalekitish kings:—Agag. In fact the (Septuagint Translation) spells it "Gog.

As yet another part of the Esther similitude, there were seven princes in the Persian King's court (Esther1:14) after Haman was elevated he became the eighth, likewise the Gog will be the eighth ruler.

Only after Gog become the eighth ruler is power given to the ten kings. Just as Haman and his ten sons tried to kill all the Jews and were themselves put to death, in the same manner all the nations that come against Israel will be destroyed. Just as the King and Esther saved the Jews, the King of Kings and his bride will also save the day for Israel (Revelation 19:11–16).

You recall how the first two total lunar eclipses on Purim occur during the celebration of Esther? The Esther connection with Gog and his identity over Iran (Persia) leads me to believe Iran will have some involvement in this coming war.

WHAT IS AN IMAM?

Dar al-Islam (Arabic: literally house of Peace) is a term used to refer to those lands under Islamic rule. In the orthodox tradition of Islam, the world is divided into two components: dar al-Islam, the *house of peace* and dar al-Harb, the *house of war*. xx Gog and the Shiite Muslims certainly fit the house of war description!

I have presented this material to show that there will be an eighth beast, led by the spirit king Gog. Most teach the antichrist will be the last world ruler. I also believe he will be a Shiite, and will proclaim and promote himself as the Twelfth Imam, the Mahdi.

THE 12ᵀᴴ IMAM

Our revolution's main mission is to pave the way for the reappearance of the Twelfth Imam, the Mahdi. - Mahmoud Ahmadinejad [Editor's Note: In the Islamic faith, the Mahdi is the ultimate savior of mankind. His appearance will usher in an era of Islamic justice and bring about the conversion of the heathen amidst flame and fire.] The Mahdi will establish Islam as the global religion, and will reign for seven years before bringing about the end of the world.

What is the 12th Imam? According to Islamic belief, an Imam is an anointed leader or ruler. Especially among the Shia beliefs an Imam is thought (though not required), to be a prayer leader or cleric when the word is capitalized. Sunnis also believe an Imam may be a prophet; Shiites believe not all prophets can be an Imam, but an Imam can also be a prophet. An Imam is said to be anointed by Allah and a perfect example of leading mankind in every way. The Shiite interpretation is that only Allah can appoint an Imam and no man has the power to do so. The 12th Imam is said to be a descendant of the Prophet Muhammad, having divine status as did each of this succession of sons. The 12th Imam is also called the Hidden Imam and the Mahdi (guided one).

WHO IS THE 12ᵀᴴ IMAM?

Within the Shiite Muslim sect (which is predominate in Iran), it is prophesied that there is coming a 12th Imam who is the great spiritual savior. This Imam is named Abu al-Qasim Muhammad or also called Muhammad al Mahdi. He is said to have been born the son of the 11th Imam, Hasan Al-Askari and his wife, the granddaughter of an Emperor. There are conflicting statements of her name being either Fatima or Nargis Khatoon. Most accounts of the story say that al Mahdi went into hiding as a child around the age of 5 years (about

13th Century). It is asserted that he has been 'in **hiding' in caves** ever since, but will supernaturally return just before the Day of Judgment. According to the Hadith the criteria for the Hidden Imam are:

He will be a descendant of Muhammad and the son of Fatima

He will have a broad forehead and pointed nose

He will return just before the end of the world

His appearance will be preceded by a number of prophetic events during 3 years of horrendous world chaos, tyranny and oppression

He will escape from Madina to Mekkah, thousands will pledge allegiance to him

He will rule over the Arabs and the world for 7 years

He will eradicate all tyranny and oppression bringing harmony and total peace

He will lead a prayer in Mekkah, during which Jesus will be at his side, and follow in

Remarkably, the 12th Imam theory plays heavily into the world's current concerns with Iran. The Shiite Muslim President of Iran, Ahmadinejad, is deeply committed to the Islamic Messiah, al Mahdi. There have been many through the years claiming to be the Hidden Imam, but Ahmadinejad believes he is yet to come. Ahmadinejad believes that he must personally prepare the world for the coming Mahdi. In order to save the world, it must be in a state of chaos and subjugation. Ahmadinejad claims he was "directed by Allah to pave the way for the glorious appearance of the Mahdi. This apocalyptic directive includes some very scary proclamations.

THE 12ᵀᴴ IMAM: WHY IS THIS ESPECIALLY IMPORTANT NOW?

While Christians look for Jesus' 2nd coming, the Jews await the Messiah and Muslims await the 12th Imam. However, of the three, Allah's designated Mahdi is the only one who demands a violent path to conquer the world. Mr. Ahmadinejad, and his cabinet, say they have a 'signed contract' with al Mahdi in which they pledge themselves to his work. What does this work involve? In light of concerns over Iran's nuclear capabilities, Mahmoud Ahmadinejad has reportedly stated Israel should be wiped off the map. He spoke to the United Nations in September '05. During that speech he claims to have been in an aura of light and felt a change in the atmosphere during which time no one present could blink their eyes. Iran's PM is also said to have spoken in apocalyptic terms and seems to relish conflict with the West whom he calls the Great Satan. This is while he proclaims he must prepare the world for the coming Mahdi by way of a world totally under Muslim control. He is working hard to bring about the world-wide horrors that must be in place for their al Mahdi to bring peace.

This notion and goal, along with a violent hatred of infidels, America and Israel reminds us of Biblical prophecies of the coming anti-Christ and the pledges of millions to a deceiving False Messiah who will claim to bring peace. Could this 12th Imam Mahdi and his servant Ahmadinejad spark the last days of the coming true Savior? xxi

In another article on the web I found the following information about the city of Jamkaran Iran. "Jamkaran, Iran (on the outskirts of Qom) is the site of the Jamkaran Mosque, a popular pilgrimage site for Shiite Muslims. The pilgrims come especially to drop a message into a **holy well**, which they hope will be received by the Imam Mahdi. One of the first acts of the government of President Mahmoud Ahmadinejad was to donate £10 million to the mosque." xxii

It is interesting to note that Gog will ascend from the bottomless pit, while the Shiites keep looking for the 12th Imam to come out of a deep cave or a well. (See Revelation 9:11).

Terrorism cannot be blamed just on "extremists". Instead, every loyal follower of Muhammad is bound by the commands of the Islam scriptures to take over the entire world, or kill all who will not convert. History and their teachings demand this conclusion. Why do governments refuse to believe what they say?

Muslims continue to kill Christians by the thousands in Algeria, Indonesia, Nigeria, Iran, etc. and into the millions (2) in Southern Sudan, because they will not convert to Islam. Muslims are burning churches down at the rate of 3000 in three years. God has obligated himself to judge people (Nations) when their sin against his chosen is ripe. **"Vengeance *is* mine; I will repay, saith the Lord (Romans 12:18b).**

MYSTERY BABYLON

> Then one of the seven angels who had the seven bowls came and spoke with me, saying, 'Come here, I will show you the judgment of the great harlot who sits on many waters, with whom the kings of the earth committed acts of immorality, and those who dwell on the earth were made drunk with the wine of her immorality.' And he carried me away in the Spirit into a wilderness; and I saw a woman sitting on a scarlet beast, full of blasphemous names, having seven heads and ten horns. The woman was clothed in purple and scarlet, and adorned with gold and precious stones and pearls, having in her hand a gold cup full of abominations and of the unclean things of her immorality, and on her forehead a name was written, a mystery, 'BABYLON THE GREAT, THE MOTHER OF HARLOTS AND OF THE ABOMINATIONS OF THE EARTH.' And I saw the woman drunk with the blood of the saints, and with the blood of the witnesses of Jesus. When I saw her, I wondered greatly. And the angel said to me, "Why do you wonder? I will tell you the mystery of the woman and

of the beast that carries her, which has the seven heads and the ten horns. (Revelation 17:1–7).

This Revelation passage teaches us that there is a "woman sitting on these seven heads (blasphemous, evil, spirit led empires) and she is identified as Mystery Babylon the Great. The city of Babylon was where the seed of man decided they could do without God, and built the tower of Babel. That is also the location where most Jews chose to remain, following the Babylonian/Persian captivity, instead of returning to the Promised Land.

The woman is identified as a religious entity composed of believers in Jehovah God, and she is called the "great harlot as she fellowships with the other satanic beasts. The woman is identified as enticing the saints (Israelites) and her off-spring (those that believe in Christ) or believers of Jehovah God, which are the seed of the sons and daughters of God. She committed fornication with the Beasts over the years, and was identified as the mother of Harlots, full of abominations, fornication, martyrs of Jesus, and that great city (Babylon) which reigns over the kings of the earth (Revelation 17:3–6). This woman also "sets on many nations and causes the kings of the earth to participate in her fornication. She represents all the apostate seed of the true God, including the Papal system of the Catholic Church and Judaism that mixes with this blasphemous beast, even to the point of accepting false religions, and their blasphemies against Jehovah God of the Bible.

It has been Satan's main goal to destroy or corrupt the good seed. We should recognize by now that Satan has used two main paths to accomplish his goal. One is by these seven beasts, and the other is by the "woman who rides the beasts By these two separate paths he wages war on God's saints both from without (political warfare) and within (think of the religious persecutions of the inquisition and all those by which nominal "Christians wage war against true Christian believers and all of God's chosen people. These two paths are founded on murder and lies.

> You are of your father the devil, and you want to do the desires of your father. He was a murderer from the beginning, and does not stand in the truth because there is no truth in him.

Whenever he speaks a lie, he speaks from his own nature, for he is a liar and the father of lies. (John 8:44).

What better way could Satan accomplish his goal than mingle with the good seed, and spread lies enticing them to do his ungodly work.

After reading an article by Dr. David Reagan in the September-October 2007 "Lamplighter magazine entitled "Anti-Semitism: Its Roots and Perseverance, xxiii it struck me that Anti-Semitism is one of, if not the root cause, of the "Woman who rides the beast? Therefore, it may be easier to understand her by looking at a few actual events that have taken place in the name of Jesus, and observe what the roots of Anti-Semitism can do.

The article explains the history of "replacement theology, the prevalent belief that **God has replaced Israel with the Church**, transferring the blessings promised to Israel to the Church. Those who adhere to "replacement theology" currently constitute the majority of professing Christians.

The Lamplighter article tells about the crusades: "In 1095 Pope Urban II called for a crusade to rid the Holy Land of its Muslim rulers. Although the prime goal of the crusade was to liberate Jerusalem from the Muslims, Jews were a secondary target. The accumulated hatreds and fears resulting from charges of deicide (the murder of God) exploded with this call to arms. The abbot of Cluny asked why Christians should travel to "the ends of the world to fight the Saracens, when we permit among us other infidels a thousand times more guilty toward Christ than the Mohammedans? Religious passion, greed, and the vulnerability of Jews led to the rise of violent mobs who murdered thousands of Jews to the cry of "Conversion or death! This behavior continued through eight additional crusades, until the 9th in 1272.

It was during the church age of the Thyatira Church that the crusades were in progress. (See Chart E). In their zeal these Crusaders were playing into the hands of the Beast, and forgetting that our fight is not against flesh and blood. They were tolerant of cults, idolatry, and immorality, and judgment was coming.

Dr. Reagan then discusses the Spanish Inquisition of 1492. Next came the reformation movement via Martin Luther, how he ended up dehumanized the Jews and his teachings were an encouragement to Adolf Hitler.

Dr. Reagan then addresses a well known current version of this eschatology: "The horror of the Holocaust tended to mute the most radical forms of anti-Semitism among Christian leaders. But in reality, anti-Semitism continues today in a new sophisticated form called anti-Zionism. Whereas anti-Semitism sought to drive the Jews from the lands where they lived, anti-Zionism refuses to accept their right to live in their own land.

A good example of the new anti-Semitism can be found in a document issued by Dr. James Kennedy's Knox Theological Seminary in 2002. It took the form of an open letter to Evangelicals concerning the land of Israel. It has since been endorsed by hundreds of theologians and pastors, including such luminaries as R. C. Sproul.

The document begins by denouncing those who teach that the Bible's promises concerning the land of Israel are being fulfilled today "in a special region or 'Holy Land,' perpetually set apart by God for one ethnic group alone. It then proceeds to proclaim that the promises made to Abraham "do not apply to any particular ethnic group, but to the church of Jesus Christ, the true Israel (emphasis added).

So, we see when the seeds of anti-Semitism are sown, they eventually produce a multitude of evil practices, from discord among brethren, to hate, to war. God and his Word do not change. "For God's gifts and the calling of God are irrevocable, (Romans 11:39). God has not rejected his people.

> Then what advantage has the Jew? Or what is the benefit of circumcision? Great in every respect. First of all, that they were entrusted with the oracles of God. What then? If some did not believe, their unbelief will not nullify the faithfulness of God, will it? May it never be! Rather, let God be found true, though every man be found a liar, as it is written, "that you may be justified in your words, and prevail when you are judged." (Romans 3:1–4)

The Jews themselves have not been exempt from riding on the Beast over the years. Even today they have misconceptions of God's plan. "Classical Reform in the last century reinterpreted the doctrine of the Messiah in two ways. First, it substituted belief in a messianic age for belief in a personal Messiah. Secondly, the messianic hope was severed from its traditional associations with a return of the exiles to Zion, these associations being viewed as too particularistic. The destruction of the Temple and the exile of the Jewish people were seen not as calamities, but as affording greater opportunities for the fulfillment of Judaism's "mission to all mankind. The whole world would become perfected and, through the example of Judaism, monotheism would be the religion of all men. This philosophy began to infiltrate not only Judaism, but Christianity also, as we have already observed. The idea that we can do it ourselves (without God) has always been around. Israel is being set up for the biggest lie ever told (by the antichrist). xxiv

> I have come in My Father's name, and you do not receive Me;
> if another comes in his own name, you will receive him. (John 5:43)

The people that make up this woman are always admonished to **"come out from among them** (II Corinthians 6:14–18). This is demonstrated in the instructions to the seven Churches. Specifically, Jesus warns all believers located in Judea to flee when they see the antichrist enter the temple (Matthew 24:15–18). Jesus warns them again in Revelation 12, how long it will be and why they must flee. They must flee because the antichrist will commence to persecute them (Revelation 12:17), and the ten Kings will hate them (Revelation 17:16). There is one last warning (by an angel from heaven) to "come out of her (Revelation 18:4), because God is about to pour out his own last bowl of wrath with earthquakes and hail (Revelation 16:19–21).

THE TRIBULATION - SEVEN TRUMPETS

WRATH OF THE LAMB

After the rapture the Lord's bride, the Church is safe. The Lamb can then pour out His wrath and accomplishes everything contained within the last seal. All the Trumpets will sound even though Jesus is in heaven with the Church. The seventh week of Daniel, the seven years of tribulation, will start and it will start immediately without a gap in time.

I believe the first three Trumpets of (Revelation 8:7–11) are the wrath of the Lamb, this is clearly stated in (Revelation 6:16). His wrath is poured out in three phases on the land, sea and waters. Jesus will pour out His wrath on the Euro Muslims, whereas he has already taken vengeance on the Arab Muslims (in this time line). Therefore, I believe these Three Trumpets are the Magog war of Ezekiel 38–39.

The terminologies used indicate nuclear warfare, but does not have to be worldwide (but will affect some of the coast land). Both the above Ezekiel and Revelation accounts indicate the raining down of fire, brimstone, burning and other nuclear conditions like poisoned water, and specialists burying the dead etc. (Similitude Joshua 8, Chart C) Iran will have the nuclear weapons at that time or have access to such weapons via Russia.

During this Magog war five out of six of the invaders will be killed on the mountains of Israel and it will take seven years to burn the armaments. I believe it will be exactly seven years from this point that the wedding feast will take place during the Feast of Tabernacles. After this decisive win **Israel will put on leaves** (prosper), as Jesus promised in Matthew 24:32. "And the nations will know that I am the LORD, the Holy One in Israel." (Ezekiel 39:7b).

After this short decisive war the future antichrist will make a covenant, concerning the Temple Mount and the temple will be rebuilt.

> And he shall confirm the covenant with many for one week: and in the midst of the week he shall cause the sacrifice and the oblation to cease, and for the overspreading of abominations he shall make it desolate, even until the consummation, and that determined shall be poured upon the desolate. (Daniel 9:27).

I believe after the previous loss (the war lost in 2008) by the Arab Muslims (the Sunni) and now the devastating blow to the Shiites in this Magog battle, the future Sunni antichrist will be in a position to step in as peace maker. He will allow Israel to keep God's "covenant and build their Temple on the Temple Mount. This will mean the Jews, Christians and the Muslims will be sharing the Temple Mount. In the midst of the seven years the antichrist will break the Covenant with Israel, and show himself as god in the new Temple.

The defeated Persian Shiites of Iran will go along with this agreement, even supporting the antichrist when he later breaks "the covenant, and they will both war against the Jews and Christians in the middle of the tribulation. (Revelation 13:7).

> Aaron Klein of WorldNetDaily reported that on Tuesday, Aug. 28, 2007 Israeli Prime Minister Ehud Olmert presented the Palestinian Authority with a formal plan in which the Jewish state would forfeit the Temple Mount — Judaism's holiest site — to Muslim control, according to top Palestinian sources.

WND reported that sources said Olmert's plan calls for the entire Temple Mount plaza to fall under Arab sovereignty; Jerusalem's Old City holy sites near the Mount to be governed by a Jewish, Christian and Muslim task force; and the Western Wall plaza below the Mount to be controlled by Israel.

Obviously the first three trumpets will be a biblical and heavenly signs. Let's review all of the lunar and solar eclipses, "the signs in the sun and moon" and what events may occur on those dates. The first trumpet may start August 5, 2014, the 9th of Av, and all three would conclude by the next total lunar eclipses on Tabernacles, Tishri 14, 5775, (October 8, 2014). Interestingly enough the scheduled Jewish Sabbath readings on these dates will be (Exodus 33:12-34), God saves Israel from Muslim invaders. The prophet reading is Ezekiel 38:18 - 39:16 describing the Magog war. Similar type readings apply to all the eclipses but for brevity I have not used them.xxv

The next total eclipse will be visible on Passover, April 4, 2015, and occur just when the **rebuilding of the Temple** begins. Later that same year there will be another eclipse on Tabernacles, September 28th, when **Temple worship starts**. The 144,000 will be preaching and teaching and marking those who respond to God's call (Revelation 9:4). Prosperity and good relations with other countries will prevail.

It is interesting to note the three solar partial eclipses are on the first day of Av historically Av is bad month for Israel. The Jews were expelled from Spain on the seventh of Av 1492. Another example Nebuchadnezzar burned the Temple on Av1. Solomon's temple burned on the ninth of Av. Etc

Observe how the first total solar eclipse of 2015 falls on the **religious New Year**, and fifteen days later there is a total lunar eclipse **Passover**. They are followed with another set in the fall with a total solar eclipse on the start of the **civil New Year**. Fifteen days later is a total lunar eclipse on the **Feast of Tabernacles**. At the very least even a skeptic must see some design in these heavenly signs! Solar and Lunar Eclipses

The following lists sums up the heavenly signs, the total lunar eclipses, *the solar eclipses*, **and the biblical signs.** (Please note the coding and grouping).

2007-March 3, Adar 14, Purim, – Identifies Iran and Gog as problem.

2008-February 21, Adar 15, Shushan Purim, – Promise of vengeance on Muslims.

2008-August, 1Av 1, partial eclipse, – Defeat of Hezbollah and Palestinians.

2009-July 22, Av 1, partial eclipse, – These next two may indicate other battles.

2010-July 11Av 1, partial eclipse, – All other eclipses are total.

2010- Dec. 21, Tevet 14, –Daniels' 70th week (7 years of tribulation in 1260 days.

2014- April 10, Nisan 10, – Biblical sign of coming dispensational change.

2014- April 15, Nisan 15, Passover, – Warning of coming tribulation and Rapture

2014- June 14, Sivan 10, Pentecost, – Possible day of the Rapture of the Church.

2014-August 5, Av 9 – Possible start Gog Magog war. (Ezekiel 38-39).

2014-October 8, Tishre 14, Succoth, Tabernacles, – God saves Israel Gog Magog.

2015-Mar. 20, Nisan 1, Religious New Year. Muslims submit to rebuilding Temple

2015-April 4, Nisan 15, Passover – Start rebuilding the Temple.

2015-September 13, Elul 29, Trumpets, – Muslims submit temple mount worship.

2015- September 28, Tishre 15, Tabernacles – Temple worship starts for Jews.

2017-June 4, Sivan 6, Pentecost, – Fourth trumpet, sign of Great Tribulation.

Note: Permission is granted by the author to copy all charts in this book for study purposes.

SIGN OF COMING WOE'S

The blowing of the **Fourth Trumpet** is also a **heavenly warning sign** (but not typical being in midst of the seven year cycle) announcing the great tribulation is about to take place and starting the transition to the next dispensation. A possible date could be June 4, 2017, Pentecost.

> The fourth angel sounded, and a third of the sun and a third of the moon and a third of the stars were struck, so that a third of them would be darkened and the day would not shine for a third of it, and the night in the same way. Then I looked, and I heard an eagle flying in mid-heaven, saying with a loud voice, "Woe, woe, woe to those who dwell on the earth, because of the remaining blasts of the trumpet of the three angels who are about to sound! (Revelation 8:12–13).

WOE 1

Let's assume the **5th Trumpet** (Revelation 9:1–12); Woe 1 sounds five months before the start of the Great Tribulation. We know that during this transition period Satan is cast to earth and **"the key of the bottomless pit was given to him."** (Revelation 9:1a).

Let me insert here that our Lord and Savior has been and is in charge of this whole plan. He is the one who gives or restricts power. He said:

> Do not be afraid; I am the first and the last, and the living One; and I was dead, and behold, I am alive forevermore, and I have the keys of death and of Hades. (Revelation 1:17b–18).

When the pit was opened locusts come out and they were given power to sting people for five months.

> And in those days men will seek death and will not find it; they will long to die, and death flees from them. (Revelation 9:6).

These locusts were **not** allowed to kill men, harm the grass or sting anyone that had the **mark of God** on their forehead (those responding to the ministry of the 144,000). This leads me to believe that Satan is assembling his forces, but the allotted 1260 days, of the antichrist, starts later (Revelation 13:5).

The king of the angels of the bottomless pit is Abaddon which means destroyer, ruin, perdition (Revelation 9:1–11). Abaddon is **Gog**, the spiritual prince of Rosh, Meshech and Tubal and I believe he exercised authority over the Medo-Persian Empire. We will learn later that he is the false prophet, and will return as the eighth Beast (the last world ruler).

At this point Jesus introduces a "little book" that contains information about the "great tribulation (Revelation 10), the same book Daniel was commanded to shut up until the time of the end (Daniel 12). John is commanded to take the "little book and eat it. It would be bitter in his stomach and he must prophesy again. In this little book we are told that it would take three and one half years (1260days) **to break the power of the holy people** (Israel). But there would be 1290 days from the abomination of desolation and anyone that waits to 1335 days would be blessed. As promised:

> Then the seventh angel sounded; and there were loud voices in heaven, saying, 'The kingdom of the world has become the

kingdom of our Lord and of His Christ; and He will reign forever and ever. (Revelation 11:15).

Two other people are now introduced and they get to witness the same 1260 days. "And I will grant authority to my two witnesses, and they will prophesy for twelve hundred and sixty days, clothed in sackcloth." (Revelation 11:3)

These men (probably Elijah and Moses or Enoch) have power to shut up the sky so that it will not rain during the time they are prophesying and they have power to turn the waters into blood and to strike the earth with every kind of plague as often as they want (Revelation 11:3–6).

Now all the combatants are in place to have a head to head spiritual battle. They include the 144,000 first fruits, those that take the mark of God, the 2 witnesses and the promised help of Michael (Daniel 12:1). The opponents are Satan and his newly released angels, and their king Abaddon (Gog), 10 kings, the one we call the antichrist and those that will take his mark (further explanation below). **The Great Tribulation can now start!**

By count the first 1260 days, of the 2520 days specified in as the seventh week of Daniel (chapter seven), will end on November.14, 2017, the 25th of Heshvan, the date in history that Jesus was consecrated in the Temple. This could be the day Satan possesses the person we call the Antichrist and will take credit for stopping the five month locust's plague.

THE GREAT TRIBULATION

WRATH OF SATAN

As prophesied the Roman Empire has deteriorated to ten toes per (Daniel 7:23–25) and as the next beast (Antichrist the seventh beast) comes to power at this time there are ten horns that he will come out of and rule over. (Revelation 13:1)

In Revelation 17:9–11, John compares the seven heads to seven kings of past world empires by saying "five have fallen. Those five fallen were (at the time John wrote), Egypt, Assyria, Babylon, Medo-Persia, and Greece. John then says "**one is**" meaning Rome and "the other is not yet come" **meaning the seventh beast** known as the Antichrist. John then describes a beast **"which was and is not, is himself also an eighth"** and is from one of the seven.

> Here is the mind which has wisdom. The **seven heads** are seven mountains on which the woman sits, and they are seven kings; **five have fallen**, **one is**, the other has not yet come; and when he comes, he must remain a little while. **The beast which was and is not, is himself also an eighth** and is one of the seven, and he goes to destruction. (Revelation 17:9-11).

Remember that Daniel's prophesies center on the last four of the above empires. The Revelation account deals with the next two kingdoms and relates to the seventh and eighth empires.

In God's view, these beasts in Revelation appear as world governments, having satanic spiritual leaders. But from the world's view, they are seen as great spiritual rulers.

(The Antichrist requires worship) as a Messiah or Mahdi is being backed up by a mighty ruler. Curiously, the (eighth beast goes out of his way to make the inhabitants of the earth worship the first beast. In this relationship, we recognize the types of Christ and the Holy Spirit being mimicked by this Antichrist and his false prophet. Later, we find the eighth beast goes to war with the seventh beast (Antichrist) and will become the eighth and last world empire.

As mentioned before, it is only during woe one and woe two when Satan is allowed to manifest his power. Satan's first order of warfare is to establish a world empire. This empire is likened to a beast too, as they all were. The first beast is likened to one rising up out of the sea, having seven heads and ten horns; and the Dragon gave him power and authority over the nations. He was given a mouth, speaking great things and blasphemies. This spokesman was given authority for 1260 days, and he is commonly referred to as the "Antichrist.

Note: Some believe and teach that this was the last world empire, and the last two empires revealed by Daniel were somehow part of this one. These people try to explain that some of the prophesies were fulfilled by A-D 70, and the rest constitute mere "apocalyptic" language that must be taken as purely symbolic or "hyperbolic language (that is, an intentional exaggeration or a figure of speech). One who takes this position is really asserting that God changed his character and no longer has a revealed plan through prophecy or specific signs of the Lord's return. One could not honestly say: "But you, brethren, are not in darkness, that the day would overtake you like a thief;" (1 Thessalonians 5:4).In fact, this would mean God has been silent for 1900 years, and the events in this article were fulfilled by AD 70 or should be interpreted as hyperbolic. I believe the common sense rule should apply, and we should speak where the Bible speaks.

THE SEVENTH BEAST

The seventh Beast (Antichrist) will be a Babylonian-type empire described in (Revelation 17:10) as, the other is yet to come and when he comes, he must continue a short time. We know his kingdom will last forty two months (Revelation 13:5). This is the beast whose fatal wound had been healed. We can see this empire now forming around Iraq, Syria, and the Middle East. As mentioned, I believe this area (and the coming Antichrist) is about to receive a fatal wound, and people will be amazed when the Antichrist takes authority as the seventh world empire a few years later.

> So the dragon was enraged with the woman, and went off to make war with the rest of her children, who keep the commandments of God and hold to the testimony of Jesus. (Revelation 12:17)

> And the dragon stood on the sand of the seashore. Then I saw a beast coming up out of the sea, having ten horns and seven heads, and on his horns were ten diadems, and on his heads were blasphemous names. And the beast which I saw was like a leopard, and his feet were like those of a bear, and his mouth like the mouth of a lion. And the dragon gave him his power and his throne and great authority. I saw one of his heads as if it had been slain, and his fatal wound was healed. And the whole earth was amazed and followed after the beast; they worshiped the dragon because he gave his authority to the beast; and they worshiped the beast, saying, 'Who is like the beast, and who is able to wage war with him?' There was given to him a mouth speaking arrogant words and blasphemies, and authority to act for forty-two months was given to him. And he opened his mouth in blasphemies against God, to blaspheme His name and His tabernacle, that is, those who dwell in heaven. It was also given to him to make war with the saints and to overcome them, and authority over every tribe and people and tongue and nation was given to him. All who dwell on the earth will worship him, everyone whose name has not been written from the foundation of the world in the book of

life of the Lamb who has been slain. (Revelation 13:1–8, Ref. Malachi 3:16).

As mentioned above, this seventh beast comes out of the present sixth Roman Empire and the ten toes, but is completely separate. He will look like a leopard, indicating his Greek heritage via General Seleucus, King of Syria. The feet like a bear indicate the eighth beast from Persia will be responsible for the movements of this Antichrist Empire (until he turns on the seventh beast). The mouth like a lion tells us he will speak with authority from Babylon, like the head of gold described in of Daniel 2.

The above text (Revelation 13:1) states this beast will come from the sea. This is probably in contrast to the eighth beast coming from the land (Iran) (Revelation 13:12), even though the four beasts (beasts three through six) of Daniel 7 were coming up from the sea (verse 3) and also "arose from the earth (verse 17). Technically, we will find the seventh empire of the Antichrist will come out of a country of the Mediterranean Sea (Israel) as he officially starts when he shows himself as God in the temple in Jerusalem. This is the same place he will come to his end on the "Holy Mountain" in Jerusalem. (Daniel 11:45).

THE ABOMINATION

As Jesus said: Therefore when you see the abomination of desolation which was spoken of through Daniel the prophet, standing in the holy place (let the reader understand), then those who are in Judea must flee to the mountains Whoever is on the housetop must not go down to get the things out that are in his house. Whoever is in the field must not turn back to get his cloak. But woe to those who are pregnant and to those who are nursing babies in those days! But pray that your flight will not be in the winter, or on a Sabbath. For then there will be a great tribulation, such as has not occurred since the beginning of the world until now, nor ever will. Unless those days had been cut short, no life would have been saved; but for the sake of the elect those days will be cut short. Then if anyone says to you, 'Behold, here is the Christ,' or 'There He is,' do not believe him. For false Christ's and false prophets will arise and will show great signs and wonders, so as to mislead, if possible, even the elect. Behold, I have told you in advance. (Matthew 24:15–25, Ref. Daniel 12:11 Mark 13:14, and 2 Thessalonians 2:4).

This Sunni Syrian Prince, on a specified day, will walk into the Temple and show himself as God.

At the request of four of the apostles, including John, Jesus dives right into the great tribulation. He lets the reader know that the abomination Daniel predicted will take place, and will be the most terrible time in history far surpassing the destruction of Jerusalem or the holocaust -- so that had God not intervened there would be no flesh left alive. There can be no doubt He is teaching about the last 1260 days. It seems to me the above text could be interrupted in the singular, a false Christ and a false prophet will appear and perform great signs.

As always when there is a dispensational change there is an opportunity to escape, just as the church will via the rapture, so Jesus says when you see this abomination everyone in Judea should flee to the mountains.

I believe this event will take place twenty five days into the 1260 day period of the great tribulation. This would make it on December 13, 2017, the twenty fifth of Kislev; the Celebration of Lights (Hanukkah). The 25th is the date the Abomination by Antiochus Epiphanes in 169 B. C. took place. (See Chart B) Daniel tell us when this happens, and the daily sacrifice is taken away, there will be 1290 days --and blessed is he who comes to the 1335th of the 1335 days (Daniel 12:12). I believe the last forty five days will be the Seventh trumpet, Woe 3, which is the seven bowls of God's wrath.

There are the ten toes (Horns) of the present waning Roman Empire (present day Middle Eastern countries).The **ten horns** were <u>on the seventh beast</u> but had no authority.

And the ten horns which you saw, and the beast, these will hate the harlot and will make her desolate and naked, and will eat her flesh and will burn her up with fire.(Revelation 17:16).

During the reign of the antichrist "Babylon the Great, the Mother of Harlots is destroyed.

These two final beasts work together for about twenty nine months making war against believers and even the great harlot.

It was also given to him to make war with the saints and to overcome them, and authority over every tribe and people and tongue and nation was given to him. All who dwell on the earth will worship him, everyone whose name has not been written from the foundation of the world in the book of life of the Lamb who has been slain.(Revelation 13:7–8, Ref. Malachi 3:16).

There is sitting on the seventh beast a woman who was identified with **Mystery Babylon**, abominations, fornication, martyrs of Jesus, and that great city which reigns over the kings of the earth (Revelation 17:3–6). This woman is apostate believers of Jehovah God which include Protestants' the Papal system of the Catholic Church and Judaism that mixed with this blasphemous beast. Summing up this fifth trumpet (Woe 1) the wrath of Satan, power is given to an individual who sets himself up as God. With the backing of another evil spirit (Gog) he makes war against the Jews and those that take the mark of God. He establishes his own mark and tries to force everyone to take it. He rules over ten kings but gives them no power.

Therefore, we have a powerful person (the antichrist) possessed by the Devil that wants to be worshiped and have people worship his image much like the old Babylon Empire. He is followed by a Medo-Persian type eighth beast, that is the false prophet, whose leader is a king from the spirit realm. The false prophet, the eighth beast, and the ten kings will hate this world religious system and they will make war against the antichrist.

The ten horns which you saw are ten kings who have not yet received a kingdom, but they receive authority as kings with the beast for one hour. These have one purpose, and they give their power and authority to the beast. (Text is speaking of the eighth beast, Revelation 17:12–13).

WRATH OF MAN - WOE 2 - THE EIGHTH BEAST

There is no women rider on this last beast because he helped the seventh beast and the ten kings destroy her. I believe this eighth beast will turn on the Sunni antichrist and declare himself as the 12th Shiite Imam (Mahdi).

> Then I saw another beast coming up out of the earth; and he had two horns like a lamb and he spoke as a dragon. He exercises all the authority of the first beast in his presence. And he makes the earth and those who dwell in it to worship the first beast, whose fatal wound was healed. He performs great signs, so that he even makes fire come down out of heaven to the earth in the presence of men. And he deceives those who dwell on the earth because of the signs which it was given him to perform in the presence of the beast, telling those who dwell on the earth to make an image to the beast who had the wound of the sword and has come to life. And it was given to him to give breath to the image of the beast, so that the image of the beast would even speak and cause as many as do not worship the image of the beast to be killed. And he causes all, the small and the great, and the rich and the poor, and the free men and the slaves, to be given a mark on their right hand or on their forehead, and he provides that no one will be able to buy or to sell, except the one who has the mark, either the name of the beast or the number of his name. (Revelation 13:11–17).

The eighth beast will make war against the Antichrist, in the process of setting up his own kingdom. Now let's look at an overview of woe 2 in (Revelation 9:13–21). There will be two hundred million combatants using armaments of fire, smoke, and brimstone. One third of mankind will be killed and this war will last a year, month, day and hour. Counting back from the end of Daniel's 1290 days, this **World War III** should start on Pentecost:

> He will pitch the tents of his royal pavilion between the seas and the beautiful Holy Mountain; yet he will come to his end, and no one will help him. (Daniel 11:45)

Zechariah 14:2 describes what will happen next.

It will come about in all the land, 'Declares the LORD,' "That two parts in it will be cut off and perish; But the third will be left in' I will bring the third part through the fire, Refine them as silver is refined, And test them as gold is tested. They will call on My name, And I will answer them; I will say, 'They are My people,' And they will say, 'The LORD is my God. (Zechariah 13:8–9).

Jerusalem is taken and the two witness are killed on Passover (2 Chronicles. 30:1–3) ending their 1260 days. This starts the typical transition to the next dispensation which will be the wrath of God.

This, Neo Medo Persian World Empire is in existence only during the transition period. This empire's starts the first order of business is to rejoice over throwing off the restraints of religion (lead by the antichrist and the two witness of God). Mankind is back to the original sin "you will be like God, not realizing that men can do nothing without the seed of God within them.

REIGN OF THE EIGHTH BEAST

When they have finished their testimony, the beast that comes up out of the abyss will make war with them, and overcome them and kill them. And their dead bodies will lie in the street of the great city which mystically is called Sodom and Egypt, where also their Lord was crucified. Those from the peoples and tribes and tongues and nations will look at their dead bodies for three and a half days, and will not permit their dead bodies to be laid in a tomb. And those who dwell on the earth will rejoice over them and celebrate; and they will send gifts to one another, because these two prophets tormented those who dwell on the earth. But after the three and a half days, the breath of life from God came into them, and they stood on their feet; and great fear fell upon those who were watching them. And they heard a loud voice from heaven saying to them, "Come up here." Then they went up into heaven in the cloud, and their enemies watched them. And in that hour there was a great earthquake, and a tenth of the city fell; seven thousand people were killed in the earthquake, and the rest were terrified and gave glory to the God of heaven. The second woe is past; behold, the third woe is coming quickly. (Revelation 11:7–14).

We are now in another typical transition period between dispensations and the eighth beast gets to reigns for "one hour" (one twenty fourth of 1290 days equaling fifty four days.

The ten horns which you saw are ten kings who have not yet received a kingdom, but they receive authority as kings with the beast for one hour. (Revelation 17:12).

As we learned earlier, in the similitude of Esther, Gog shares the wealth with the ten nations and it is nearing time for the stone to strike the ten.

The head of that statue was made of fine gold, its breast and its arms of silver, its belly and its thighs of bronze, its legs of iron, its feet partly of iron and partly of clay. You continued looking until a stone was cut out without hands, and it struck the statue on its feet of iron and clay and crushed them. (Daniel 2:32–34).

Near the time the two witnesses are taken to heaven the 144,000 are also taken. They meet on Mt. Zion and were taken before the throne, and they will follow the Lamb wherever He goes. (Revelation 14:1–5). Reading on we find God will not permit the earth to be without a witness.

And I saw another angel flying in mid-heaven, having an eternal gospel to preach to those who live on the earth, and to every nation and tribe and tongue and people; and he said with a loud voice, "Fear God, and give Him glory, because the hour of His judgment has come; worship Him who made the heaven and the earth and sea and springs of waters." (Revelation 14:6–7).

True to His character and His pattern God removes his own people (before He pours out His wrath, just as Jesus removed the Church before He poured out his wrath. I believe those that had the mark of God, even those that died during the tribulation, are raptured at the end of this transition period.

> Then I saw another sign in heaven, great and marvelous, seven angels who had seven plagues, which are the last, because in them the wrath of God is finished. And I saw something like a sea of glass mixed with fire, and those who had been victorious over the beast and his image and the number of his name, standing on the sea of glass, holding harps of God. And they sang the song of Moses, the bond-servant of God, and the song of the Lamb, saying, "Great and marvelous are Your works, O Lord God, the Almighty; Righteous and true are Your ways, King of the nations!"(Revelation 15:1–3).

> Verses 5-8 continue with the seven angels with seven golden bowls full of the wrath of God!

Summing up, the eighth Beast turned on the antichrist on a Pentecost and started WW III that was prophesied to last a year, a month, a day and an hour (391days), thus fulfilling the 1290 days prophesied by Daniel. One hour after the fulfillment of these prophesies God takes over with His wrath.

Woe 2 -- the eighth Beast lead by Gog -- will overcome the seventh Beast lead by the antichrist on Passover of the 1260th day of the antichrist's reign. The two witnesses are killed, and taken to heaven after three and one half days. The armies from the east may be on the move toward Jerusalem at this same time and this new Medo-Persian, Shiite empire (Russia-Iran) will be more than willing to continue WW III even to the point of destroying mankind; but for God's merciful intervention.

You may have noticed in Chart B the last day allotted to the antichrist falls on the fifteenth of Iyar, one month after the normal Passover. This is due to the fact seven extra months are inserted into the Hebrew calendar every nineteen years. Since the antichrist is also a typology an "anti-typology) of Christ, it is appropriate the he should likewise meet his end on Passover, which he does. God anticipated this by previously authorizing the postponement of Passover one month. (2 Chronicles 30:1–3, Numbers 9:9–11). Certainly by now there should be no doubt God has a plan, with a precise fulfillment of days. I have run this pattern on two other years and it works. That within itself speaks of design and a designer.

By design the Sea of Glass Rapture will probably take place on the specified day of first fruits "Pentecost", even though the transition period to this rapture will be shorter. This will leave thirty days for the angel to preach **"the eternal gospel** to all that live on the earth before God pours out His Wrath.

> Before leaving this area I should also mention those that had overcome the mark of the beast via the sea of glass rapture: "They held **harps given them** by God and sang the song of Moses the servant of God and the song of the Lamb (Revelation 15:1–3).

The song of Moses is found in the fifteenth chapter of Exodus. There is no logical reason for anyone to assume this is figurative language as some do. Besides, who is authorized or has enough intestinal fortitude to declare what it means other than what it says? They had "harps which necessarily infer there are instruments of worship in heaven. God of course commanded to be worshiped with instruments in (2 Chronicles 29:25), and God doesn't change. He has not rescinded that order. All believers know Jesus took the curse of the law on the tree, but use of instruments is not and never was part of the "curse.. We further know that during David's time, he had musicians and writers on duty twenty four hours a day. This was taking place while there was no veil between the Ark of the Covenant and those worshiping God; the Ark of the Covenant was simply under a tent. All this is a similitude (type) of the Christian's relationship to God in this age of Grace. We have a right to approach God's throne in the same manner. That grace extends to all who call on the name of the Lord (Romans 10:8–13). It is best if we are not found judging each other on what feast days we observe.

Accept him whose faith is weak, without passing judgment on disputable matters. One man's faith allows him to eat everything, but another man, whose faith is weak, eats only vegetables. The man who eats everything must not look down on him who does not, and the man who does not eat everything must not condemn the man who does, for God has accepted him. Who are you to judge someone else's servant? To his own master he stands or falls. And he will stand, for the Lord is able to make him stand.

One man considers one day more sacred than another; another man considers every day alike. Each one should be fully convinced in his own mind. He who regards one day as special, does so to the Lord. He who eats meat, eats to the Lord, for he gives thanks to God; and he who abstains, does so to the Lord and gives thanks to God. Or none of us lives to himself alone and none of us dies to himself alone. If we live, we live to the Lord; and if we die, we die to the Lord. So, whether we live or die, we belong to the Lord.

For this very reason, Christ died and returned to life so that he might be the Lord of both the dead and the living. You, then, why do you judge your brother? Or why do you look down on your brother? For we will all stand before God's judgment seat. (Romans 14:1–10).

Over the last twenty to thirty years what is commonly referred to as Messianic worship has come to be common in church worship. In 1984 Micah and Shoshana Harrari reestablished the ten string harp of David. It was said of the Rabbis when this happened the coming of the Messiah would be near. http://www.harrariharps.com/files/home.php

WRATH OF GOD - WOE 3

As promised God cuts this transition short and exactly one hour past the 1290 specified by Daniel the seventh trumpet blows and the wrath of God starts.

> Then the seventh angel sounded; and there were loud voices in heaven, saying, 'The kingdom of the world has become the kingdom of our Lord and of His Christ; and He will reign forever and ever. (Revelation 11:15).

The first bowl of God's wrath is against man, causing boils to afflict those with the mark of the beast; then against the ocean; then the rivers and springs; then the earth. The fifth is a heavenly sign of total darkness on the kingdom of the beast. With the sixth bowl God permits the Euphrates River to dry up.

> The sixth angel poured out his bowl on the great river, the Euphrates; and its water was dried up, so that the way would be prepared for the kings from the east. And I saw coming out of the mouth of the dragon and out of the mouth of the beast and out of the mouth of the false prophet, three unclean spirits like frogs; for they are spirits of demons, performing signs, which

go out to the kings of the whole world, to gather them together for the war of the great day of God, the Almighty. 'Behold, I am coming like a thief. Blessed is the one who stays awake and keeps his clothes, so that he will not walk about naked and men will not see his shame.' And they gathered them together to the place which in Hebrew is called Har-Magedon. (Revelation 16:12–16).

Jesus spoke of this time in (Matthew 24:22-27) His coming would be like the lighting, everyone will see Him coming. This will be the time Jesus returns:

Then that lawless one will be revealed whom the Lord will slay with the breath of His mouth and bring to an end by the appearance of His coming; (2Thessalonians 2:8).

Now this will be the plague with which the LORD will strike all the peoples who have gone to war against Jerusalem; their flesh will rot while they stand on their feet, and their eyes will rot in their sockets, and their tongue will rot in their mouth.(Zechariah 14:12)

This would be the month of Av, and the ninth is the fast of Av the day of mourning, and the 15th is one of the best in Jewish history. (Revelation 19) gives a vivid description of Christ on a white horse coming to judge and make war:

And the armies which are in heaven, clothed in fine linen, white and clean were following Him on white horses. From His mouth comes a sharp sword, so that with it He may strike down the nations, and He will rule them with a rod of iron; and He treads the wine press of the fierce wrath of God, the Almighty. (Revelation 19:14–15)

All those that have white robes get white horses also and are privileged to observe the culmination of this great plan. Witnessing the beast and false prophet are cast into the lake of fire and Satan is cast into the bottomless pit for 1000 years. What a great show down! But not to be compared to the coming glory!

THE JUDGMENT OF THE HARLOT

Then the seventh angel poured out his bowl upon the air, and a loud voice came out of the temple from the throne, saying, 'It is done'. And there were flashes of lightning and sounds and peals of thunder; and there was a great earthquake, such as there had not been since man came to be upon the earth, so great an earthquake was it, and so mighty. The great city was split into three parts, and the cities of the nations fell. Babylon the great was remembered before God, to give her the cup of the wine of His fierce wrath. And every island fled away, and the mountains were not found. And huge hailstones, about one hundred pounds each, came down from heaven upon men; and men blasphemed God because of the plague of the hail, because its plague was extremely severe. (Revelation 16:17-21).

The above verses tell us it will be the seventh bowl of God's wrath that will judge all of "Babylon the Great but (Revelation 18–19:3), gives the details of God judging the great harlot.

The very day God's wrath is complete is on the first day of the month of Elul and the 40 days of teshuva (returning or repenting) starts. As it was with the counting of the Omer by the church, in like manner Israel will be counting the 40 days of repentance, which will culminate on Yom Kipper when they too will look on their Messiah whom they pierced.

DAYS OF AWE – FEAST OF TRUMPETS

Jesus again sums up what will take place immediately after the tribulation (Matthew 24:29–30). How these signs of God's wrath will take place and how all the nations will mourn seeing His return with power. But notice His next statement.

> And He will send forth His angels with A GREAT TRUMPET and THEY WILL GATHER TOGETHER His elect from the four winds, from one end of the sky to the other. (Matthew 24:31).

What he is saying is every Jew and Israelite on earth will be gathered together.

> Then there will be two men in the field; one will be taken and one will be left. 'Two women will be grinding at the mill; one will be taken and one will be left.' Therefore be on the alert, for you do not know which day your Lord is coming. (Matthew 24:40–42).

This is speaking of the Feast of Trumpets (Yom Teruah) and of course as Jesus mentions in verse 36 **"that day and hour no one knows.** In Hebrew thought this is true because the Jewish New Year does not begin on a set calendar date, but when the new moon becomes visible as determined by the testimony of two Levitical witnesses. Also, in the text the ingathering of an individual could come at any moment during this Feast of Trumpets (ingathering). Christ further explains the conditions that will exist at that time (in verses 5-51) through the parable of the faithful servant and the evil servant.

This event is not to be confused with the rapture, where the believers are caught up and changed. This is an ingathering by angels, and it is part of the grafting of Israel back into the olive tree. It is the very thing the Lord has been working for. Nor is it to be confused with thinking just the Jews are all of Israel or the Church has replaced Israel. On the contrary this will be a physical gathering of the "lost tribes of Israel and the Jews. Prophecies about Israel will make no sense without this understanding.

> And He will lift up a standard for the nations And assemble the banished ones of Israel, And will gather the dispersed of Judah From the four corners of the earth. (Isaiah 11:12).

> Say to them, 'Thus says the Lord GOD', "Behold, I will take the sons of Israel from among the nations where they have gone, and I will gather them from every side and bring them into their own land; and I will make them one nation in the land, on the mountains of Israel; and one king will be king for all of them; and they will no longer be two nations and no longer be divided into two kingdoms." (Ezekiel 37:21–22).

> For thus says the Lord GOD, "Behold, I Myself will search for My sheep and seek them out As a shepherd cares for his herd in the day when he is among his scattered sheep, so I will care for My sheep and will deliver them from all the places to which they were scattered on a cloudy and gloomy day. (Ezekiel 34:11–12).

> As a shepherd looks after his scattered flock when he is with them, so will I look after my sheep? I will rescue them from all the places where they were scattered on a day of clouds and darkness. I will bring them out from the nations and gather them from the countries and I will bring them into their own land. I will pasture them on the mountains of Israel, in the ravines and in all the settlements in the land (Ezekiel 34:11–13, NIV).

This indeed will be an awesome event when all these people are camped all over Israel. Those that are brought in by angels and those that were left will be in amazement when they realize they are relatives. Bringing the outcasts of Israel and the dispersed of Judah to gather, from all over the world, to the mountains, ravines and settlements of Israel, has never occurred in history. Now that all are assembled, on the 10th of Tishri, the prophetic Feast of God "**Yom Kipper** will be fulfilled when they see their Messiah.

> And I will pour out on the house of David and the inhabitants of Jerusalem a spirit of grace and supplication. They will look on me, the one they have pierced, and they will mourn for him as one mourns for an only child, and grieve bitterly for him as one grieves for a firstborn son. (Zechariah 12:10).

Thus the "Days of Awe, what words can describe it better? What an amazing event. Now one can read (Romans 9–11) and understand what God had planned all along. God did not leave us without a plan for 1900 years, as some teach. But His plans are not over. There is one more Feast to fulfill, "the Feast of Tabernacles (Succoth), which means "God with us".

DAYS OF JOY - FEAST OF TABERNACLES

Now we come to the "Days of Rejoicing, also known as the Feast of Tabernacles and the wedding supper of the Lamb.

Let us rejoice and be glad and give the glory to Him, for the marriage of the Lamb has come and His bride has made herself ready. It was given to her to clothe herself in fine linen, bright and clean; for the fine linen is the righteous acts of the saints. Then he said to me, "Write, 'Blessed are those who are invited to the marriage supper of the Lamb.' And he said to me, these are true words of God." (Revelation 19:7–9).

Those that were wise virgins (that had accepted their (Messiah) will be given a wedding garment along with an invitation to attend the wedding feast. I have been through three weddings with my daughters and I understand the necessity of planning. Believe me; everyone invited knew when the weddings were to take place, so will we.

The feast will start on the full moon the fifteenth of Tishri (Tuesday, September 21, 2021). There will be a coronation for our King. As we celebrate this wedding feast our Lord and Savior will keep His promise to eat bread and drink wine with us. "For I tell you, I will not eat it again until it finds fulfillment in the kingdom of God" (Luke 22:15). After 7 days of celebrating no one will want to leave so the host will extend the feast one more day. Then as the guests leave the nations will be charged to return to Jerusalem every year, "to worship the King the Lord of hosts, and to keep the Feast of Tabernacles" (Zechariah 14:16). What Joy!

THE MILLENNIAL REIGN

Soon after the start of the 1000 year reign there are some judgments that take place. There has already been the **judgment for the bride of Christ** at the rapture (2 Corinthians 5:10). Jesus now addresses the judgment of the tribulation (unprepared) **believers** with the parable of wise and foolish virgins as they were not allowed to go to the wedding feast (Matthew 25:1-13). He then continues with the **judgment of Israel** based on the parable of the talents resulting in, "throw that worthless servant outside, into the darkness, where there will be weeping and gnashing of teeth (Matthew 25:30). Finally there will be a **judgment of the nations** based on how they treated the Jews.

> When the Son of Man comes in his glory, and all the angels with him, he will sit on his throne in heavenly glory. All the nations will be gathered before him, and he will separate the people one from another as a shepherd separates the sheep from the goats. He will put the sheep on his right and the goats on his left." (Matthew 25:31-32).

> Then He will answer them, 'Truly I say to you, to the extent that you did not do it to one of the least of these, you did not do

it to Me.' these will go away into eternal punishment, but the righteous into eternal life. (Matthew 25:45–46).

Thus says the LORD, 'I will return to Zion and will dwell in the midst of Jerusalem. Then Jerusalem will be called the City of Truth, and the mountain of the LORD of hosts will be called the Holy Mountain. (Zechariah 8:3).

And the LORD will be king over all the earth; in that day the LORD will be the only one, and His name the only one. (Zechariah 14:9) Praise God!

AFTER THE MILLENNIUM

Revelation 20–22), tells us the rest of the story. After the thousand years have expired Satan will be released from his prison and recruit Gog and his followers to go out and deceive the nations. God will give all those born on earth during the millennium a choice of whom they will serve. Fire then come from God out of heaven and devour all the bad seed, and the beast and the false prophet will be cast into the lake of fire forever. There will be a **white throne judgment of all the dead who have not already been judged**. This is the final judgment and not to be confused with the above judgments that take place at the start of the millennial reign.

Finally all things will be made new, a new earth and a New Jerusalem for eternity. **Choose you this day whom you will serve!**

Conclusion

I pray this writing has given an overview of God's plan, knowing full well other details could have been added, and admitting some could be wrong. I do believe this is the heart of God and His overall plan. Any theology or doctrine that tries to replace it is from the heart of man and powers of darkness, constituting a futile effort to frustrate the purposes and promises of God! God cannot lie. God cannot change. **Jesus is the only way to God** (Titus 1:2, Malachi 3:6, and John 4:6).

> For to this end Christ died and lived again, that He might be Lord both of the dead and of the living. But you, why do you judge your brother? Or you again, why do you regard your brother with contempt? For we will all stand before the judgment seat of God. For it is written, "AS I LIVE, SAYS THE LORD, EVERY KNEE SHALL BOW TO ME, AND EVERY TONGUE SHALL GIVE PRAISE TO GOD." (Romans 14:9–12).

CHART A

Chart A - The Heavenly Signs - Seals - Trumpets – Bowls

Opening of Seal	First Seal White Horse	Second Seal Red Horse	Third Seal Black Horse	Fourth Seal Pale Horse	Fifth Seal Souls Under Altar	Sixth Seal 1st Heavenly Sign	After Seventh Seal Silence
"Do not weep! See, the Lion of the tribe of Judah, the Root of David, has triumphed (Revelation 5:5) He is able to open the scroll and its seven seals."	Christ the Alpha on a white horse. Bow and Crown Revelation 6:1 Hos. 1:5 Zech. 9:13 For I have bent Judah. My Bow, Fitted the bow with Ephraim.	Takes Peace from earth. Great sword Revelation 6:5-6 Britain prepares the land for Israel World War I The Great War. 1914 -1918	Famine, do not hurt oil or wine Revelation 6:7-8 22 Million Die 1922 -1944	World War II Power over ¼ earth to kill with sword→ hunger→ death→ & beasts = Present days. Rev. 6:7-8 War prepared Israel for the land	Slain for the word of God. Cry how long, to avenge our blood. Revelation 6:9-11 Israel Prays at the Western wall, under the alter. 1967 War	Great Earth Quake Sun black as sack cloth, moon as blood, stars fall. The sky receded like a scroll. Revelation 6:12-17 Luke 21:28 -lift up your heads, because your redemption is drawing near."	Silence one half hour = about 50 days. Trumpets prepare to Blow. Revelation 8:1-2 144,000 Marked 1st Fruits Offering Revelation 7:3-4 Church Ruptured Revelation 7:9-17

Total ~ 120 Years --------- Matthew 24:37 "But as it was in the days of Noah, so it will be at the coming of the Son of Man --------- Transition period before the rapture –

Wrath of Lamb	First Trumpet	Second Trumpet	Third Trumpet	Fourth Trumpet 2nd Heavenly Sign	Fifth Trumpet Wrath of Satan	Sixth Trumpet Wrath of Man	Seventh Trumpet
Revelation 6:16 Out of the Seventh Seal comes, the Seven Trumpet Judgments, Bowls and every other recorded event to Christ's return	1/3 Trees, all the Grass burned. Revelation 8:7 Nuclear War, described in Ezekiel 38-39. "So will I make my holy name known in the midst of my people Israel; and I will not let them pollute my holy name any more; and the heathen shall know that I am the LORD, The Holy One in Israel." Ezekiel 39:7	1/3 if creatures die in Sea, 1/3 ships. Revelation 8:8-9	1/3 of all water poisoned Revelation 8:10-11	1/3 of Sun, Moon, & Stars darkened Revelation 8:12 Sign of The Great Tribulation about to start.	Woe One! Satan Cast Down. Scorpion's Sting. Revelation 9:1-12 War against believers Antichrist shows him self as god. Starts his 1260 days. Rev. 13:5	Woe Two! Great Tribulation War kill 1/3 mankind Revelation 9:13-21 War against the antichrist.	"The kingdom of the world has become the kingdom of our Lord and of his Christ, and he will reign for ever and ever." (Revelation 11:15) God shorten the days by with direct intervention.

7 Years tribulation→ -------- Nuclear war, probably a very short war ------ Transition reign of antichrist—Last 5 Months ---Year, Month, Day, Hour—God takes over w/wrath

Wrath of God	First Bowl	Second Bowl	Third Bowl	Fourth Bowl	Fifth Bowl 3rd Heavenly Sign	Sixth Bowl	Seventh Bowl
Woe Three! The seven bowl judgments of God wrath come out of the seventh trumpet	Boils affect those with Mark of Antichrist. Revelation 16:2	Sea of Blood everything in ocean dies. Revelation 16:3	Rivers and Springs turn to blood. Revelation 16:4-7	Heat from Sun scorches all mankind. Revelation 16:8-9	Total Darkness Revelation 16:10-11 Sign of the Lord's Soon Return	River Euphrates dried up, and the kings are gathered for Armageddon Revelation 16:12-16	Great Earthquake, Great Hail. Revelation 16:17-21 Christ the Omega can now returns on a white horse. With saved.

Per Daniel 12:11-12, There will be 1290 days, from the time the daily sacrifice is taken away. Then 45 days of Gods wrath (total 1335 days). After which Armageddon, binding Satan and the regathering of Israel will take place, then the second coming. Culminating the 10th of Tishri (Atonement) followed by Tabernacles (God with us). →

CHART B

Chart B - Possible End Time Scenario, Starting 2007					
Date	Day	Days	Date	Secular Event / Sign	Religious Event
Present Day - Warning Signs of a coming Dispensational change. Luke 21:25-28 – **Age of Grace**					
Mar. 3, 2007, 5767	Sat.		Adar 13	Eclipse-Israel seeks God Signs in the moon Like 25:25	Fast of Esther 6 Eclipses - feast days.
Feb. 21, 2008, 5768	Sat.		Adar 15	Eclipse – Vengeance on Arab Muslims	Shushan Purim
Sept. 30, 2008, 5769	Tues.		Tishri 1	Land rests	Start Sabbatical year
Apr. 10, 2014, 5774	Thurs		Nisan 10	VI **Sign** of His coming. Luke 25:27, Rev. 6;12-17	10TH Nisan, Day of Biblical Signs
Apr. 15, 2014	Tues.		Nisan 15	**Full Moon Eclipse**	Passover
June 4, 2014	Wed.	1/	Sivan 6	Jewish Pentecost - Times of Gentiles ends Lk.21:24	**Shavuot** - 70th wk starts 144,000 first fruits
June 8, 2014	Sun	4 /	Sivan 10	Rapture-Pentecost Lk21:28, Rev.7:3-4	Sunday after 7 Sabbaths Commanded count days
Tribulation - In this Dispensation one must take the mark of God to be saved – **Wrath of the Lamb**.					
July 15 2014	Tues.		Tammuz 17	Maastricht Treaty-confirm 7yr	Fast of Tammuz
Aug. 5, 2014, 5774	Tues.		Av 9	Trumpets I-III Vengeance European Muslims	Ezekiel 38-39 War Russia attacks Israel
Oct. 8, 2014 5775	Wed.		Tishri 14	**Full Moon Eclipse** Israel saved from Gog	Tabernacles Peace Reigns
Apr.4, 2015, 5776	Sat.		Nisan 15	**Eclipse** -Start temple	Passover
Sept. 28,2015, 5776	Mon.		Tishri 15	**Eclipse** Temple worship starts	Tabernacles
June 4, 2017 5777	Sun.		Sivan 6	Trumpet IV, 1/3 Sun, Moon, & Stars darkened	**Pentecost** - Sign of Great Tribulation.
July 11,2017, 5777	Tues.		Tammuz 17	Trumpet V, Woe I Locust Plague starts. Last 5 months.	Satan, Cast to earth. Idol placed in Temple
Nov.14, 2017,5778	Tues.	1260/	Heshvan 25	**Great Tribulation** – Antichrist in Temple.	Jesus consecrated in Temple, 30 days old.
Reign of Antichrist -Great Tribulation – **Wrath of Satan**					
Dec 7, 2017	Thru.		Kislev 19	Locust Plague ends	**Antichrist** take credit
Dec. 13, 2017	Wed.	/1	Kislev 25	**Abomination of Desolation** Antiochus Ephienes. Daniels 1335 day count down starts.	**Feast of Lights** Daily sacrifice stops. Matt. 24:15
May 31, 2020, 5780	Fri. Sun.		Sivan 8	Trumpet VI, Woe 2 World War - 391 days	**Pentecost** by Christian count
Apr. 27, 20215781	Tues.	2520/	Iyar 15	Antichrist?? ½ city captive. 2 witnesses die.	Daniel 70th wk ends Passover 2nd month
Reign of 8th Beast - The eighth beast takes Reigns from the Antichrist - **Wrath of Man**					
May 1, 2021, 5781	.Fri.		Iyar 18	Two, Witness raised. Great earthquake.	Tenth of city & 7000 killed.
May 16, 2021	Sun.		Sivan 5	Sea of Glass Rapture	Pentecost- Christian
June 25, 2021	Fri	/1290	Tammuz 15		War ends
Reign of God - Kingdom of Our God one hour into next day – **Wrath of God**					
June 26 2021, 5781	Sat.	/1291	Tammuz 16	391 days Woe 2 ends. **Woe 3** Trumpet VII , Rev. 11:15	Boils - affect those w/mark of Antichrist.
July 18, 2021	Sun.		Av 9	Armageddon	
Aug. 9, 2021, 5781	Mon.	/1335	Elul 1	Wrath of God ends. 40 Days of penitence starts.	Period of Repentance Count 40 days
Sept. 7, 2021, 5782	Tue.		Tishri 1	Ingathering, all Israel.	Trumpets
Sept. 16	Thurs		Tishri 10	Israel looks on Him.	Atonement
Sept. 21	Tues.		Tishri 15	Dwell to gather. Tabernacles –God with us.	
Sept. 23	Thurs		Tishri 17	Wedding Feast on 3rd day. This day	

CHART C

Chart C - Joshua Possessing the Land – Seven Trumpets			
Revelation		**Joshua**	
First Three Years of Tribulation - War Against Israel			
Trumpets 1-3, Three phase, Magog world war	Five out of six killed in attach.	Lose first battle. Win three-phase battle of Ai.	What will you do for your great name? (7:9)
Hail and fire, 1/3 trees and all grass burned up, burning star w1/3 water.	God justifies his name.	Ai "the ruin" destroyed, by fire	Slew all the inhabitants
Christ's wrath against false claim to Jehovah	Muslim religion, false Judaism, destroyed.	Joshua gets revenge for defeat.	Crucified king of Ai
Jews build Temple and worship.	Jews receive heart of flesh. Hope renewed.	Joshua builds an alter	Renews covenant
Many receive the mark of God	144,000 bring many into covenant relationship	Joshua makes covenant with Gibeonites	Gentiles come under protection of Israel.
The Great Tribulation - War against the Saints -Woe 1			
Trumpet 4, 1/3 Moon Sun & Stars darkened Woe to the inhabitants	Moon sign to Israel Start of Transition	Sun, Moon stand still	Sun sign to Amorites
Trumpet 5, Woe 1 Locusts from pit	Can not harm believers Harm only the enemy.	Hail from heaven	Enemy killed
Antichrist makes War against Saints. "king of Jerusalem"	Antichrist kills all who will not worship him. Successful to wrath.	Adoni-Zedek "lord of righteousness" king of Jerusalem, and 4 kings. War w/covenant people	Enemy killed, with great Slaughter
God hides Jews	Safe place in desert 1260 days.	Five Kings hide in cave	Crucified and buried in cave.
Babylon the great city burned, "great harlot" Drunk with blood of saints. Burned (17-19)	Roman burned. False claims, using name of Christ. God avenged.	Gideon seat of ancient sanctuary, called "the great high place" (1 Kings 3:4)	City of Gideon comes under attach. Not destroyed.
Great World War Against Antichrist - Woe 2			
Trumpet 6, Woe 2, 8th beast war with antichrist	Antichrist looses. 1/3 men killed	War against Jabin King of Hazor.	Utterly destroyed. Northern Conquest.
World War III	The number of the mounted troops was two hundred million. (9-16)	Army of Jabin "one who is intelligent" and Kings.	As many people as sand of the seashore, and may horses. (11:4)
City of Babylon burned (14:7)	The head of anti God world system.	Hazor "enclosed place" burned.	Formerly head of all those kingdoms (11:10)
God Takes Control - Woe 3			
Trumpet 7, Woe 3, wrath of God.	God takes control. Gives land to Israel.	Joshua utterly destroyed them. (11:21)	Gave land to Israel as inheritance. (11:23)

The Sign of Your Coming?

CHART D

Chart D – Transitions between Dispensations

Transitions Purposes	Sign and Date Starting Transition	Old System Stops	Between Old and New	New System Starts New Age	Transition To
1 - Nation Chosen by God.	Darkness, possibly on the 10th of Nisan.	Israel's deliverance, from Egypt day after Passover 15th of Nisan	Crossing of Red Sea. Travel to Mt. Sinai.	God makes covenant with the nation of Israel Pentecost, 6th Sivan	Covenant with God.
2 - Physical Nation Nation of God	Jordan River dries up 10th of Nisan.	Manna stops, day after Passover. 15th of Nisan.	Young men circumcised Captain of the Lord's host, appears to Joshua.	Captain of Lord's host, takes Jericho. Pentecost, 6th Sivan?	Promised Land Start of new life.
3 - Nation Chosen by Christ.	Jesus rides into Jerusalem presented as King. Chosen as Lamb of God Zech. 9:9. 10th of Nisan.	Passover (Crucifixion) Buried evening start of 15th of Nisan.	Christ teaches 40 days. The ascension. Believers wait for power.	Pentecost, 6th Sivan Birth of Spiritual Israel. Kingdom not of world.	Covenant with Christ New and better covenant. Holy Spirit empowerment Kingdom of heaven with in. (Spiritual not earthly)
4 - Spiritual Nation Holy Nation	6th Seal. Sun black as sack cloth, moon as blood, stars 10th of Nisan?	144,000 marked. Silence from heaven. 15th of Nisan?	Silence! 144,000 marked Church waits for shout. Just as Rahab waited.	Church raptured, on Pentecost. 144,000 preach.	Promised Land Start of new life, heaven. Start of tribulation.

The seven years of tribulation starts here. –Transition is a period of time that takes place between dispensations. When God changes how he will deal with nations.
Wrath of the Lamb = Trumpets 1-3 last a few days – to the Ezek. 38-39 war which will bring peace & restore the land to Israel. 144,000 preach.

5 - Kingdom of Satan	4th Trumpet, 1/3 of sun, moon & stars darkened. 10th Tishri. Atonement	Satan cast down; God of this world is with man. 15th Tishri, Tabernacles	Gog released, locusts given power to torment five months. Two witnesses preach.	Satan stands in temple. Day Jesus consecrated. Start 1260 days. Matt. 24:15, (not Dan. 12:11) 25th Cheshvan	Reign of Antichrist Great Tribulation Antichrist war against Believers. Israel broken.

Wrath of Satan = Woe 1 = 5th Trumpet = War against believers. Those that had taken the mark of God via the 144,000
Wrath of Man = Woe 2 = 6th Trumpet = 391 day war against the Antichrist. No heavenly sign from God. No transition.

6 - Rule of Man	Jerusalem Surrounded. 10th of Nisan	Jerusalem taken. Antichrist, 2 witnesses killed. 1260 days up. 15th of Nisan	Eighth Beast, one hour. Zechariah 13:8-9, 2/3 Israel struck down. 1/3 brought through the fire. ½ city captive.	Pentecost, sea of glass Rapture. 1290 days up. God takes control.	Reign of 8th Beast Total Destruction No flesh would be left Unless God intervenes.

Wrath of God = Woe 3 = 7th Trumpet = Seven Bowls. 45 days ends 1335 days after Antichrist go in the Temple. Armageddon follows.

7 - Kingdom of God	Look upon me the a-z whom they have pierced. 10th Tishri. Atonement.	Tabernacles, God with us. 15th Tishri.	Wedding Feast. 17th Tishri. Great day of rejoicing 21st Tishri	Coronation of Christ Last great day 22nd Tishri.	1000 Year Reign of Christ Great Peace

One thousand year reign.

8 - Rule of God	Jerusalem surrounded. 10th Nisan?	Fire from heaven Satan Cast, Lake of Fire	Great White Throne Judgment	New heaven and Earth	Reign of God Eternal Life

God has always given a warning sign and a way of escape. These signs assure us he will not change his pattern for the rapture of the church! Luke 21:25-28

CHART E

Chart E - Seven Churches of Revelation

Church - Meaning	Commendation	Criticism	Instruction	Promise	Church Age	Dates (A.D.)
Ephesus Desired one	Rejects evil, perseveres, has patience	Love for Christ no longer fervent	Do the works you did at first	The tree of live	Apostolic	< 100
Smyrna Myrrh (Death)	Gracefully bears	None	Be faithful until death	The crown of life	Persecution	100 - 313
Pergamos Mixed Marriage	Keeps the faith of Christ	Tolerates immorality, idolatry	Repent	Hidden manna and a stone with a new name	Imperial Church	313 - 590
Thyatira Semiramis (Babylon)	Love, service, faith, patience is greater than at first	Tolerates cult of idolatry and immorality	Judgment coming; keep the faith	Rule over nations and receive morning star	Papacy	590 - Tribulation
Sardis Remnant	Some have kept the faith	Dead church, will not know hour of coming	Repent strengthen what remains	Faithful honored and clothed in white	Reformation	1517 - Tribulation
Philadelphia Brotherly Love	Perseveres inn the faith	None	Keep the faith	Keep you from the hour of trial; be in New Jerusalem	Missionary Church	1730 – Rapture
Laodicea People Rule	None	Indifferent	Be zealous and repent	Share Christ's throne	Tribulation Church	7 yr. Tribulation- 2nd Coming

HEBREW CALENDARS

Hebrew Calendars			
The Civil Calendar		The Festival Calendar	
1. Tishri (Ethanim)	7. Nisan (Aviv)	1. Nisan (Aviv)	7. Tishri (Ethanim)
2. Cheshvan	8. Iyar (Zif)	2. Iyar (Zif)	8. Cheshvan (Bul)
3. Kislev	9. Sivan	3. Sivan	9. Kislev
4. Tevet	10. Tammuz	4. Tammuz	10. Tevet
5. Shevat	11. Av	5. Av	11. Shevat
6. Adar	12. Elul	6. Elul	12. Adar

NOTES

i Arnold L. Beizer, If You Don't Ask You Will Never Know. Sword Publications, 1990.
ii The works of Josephus. Hendrickson Publishers, 1994. Book 11, chapter 5, 4.148.
iii The works Josephus. Hendrickson Publishers, 1994. Book 11, chapter 5, 2.133.
iv Judah Gribetz .The Timetables of Jewish History. Simon & Schuster. 378.
v Britannica 1996. volume 4, 675.
vi Judah Gribetz, Edward Greenstein and Regina Stein. The Timetables of Jewish History. Simon & Schuster, 1993. 404.
vii Sir Robert Anderson. The Coming Prince. Hodder & Stoughton.
viii Temple Institute. Http://templeinstitute.org.
ix NEIC, 2008. http://earthquake.usgs.gov/regional/neic/.
x Robert Roy Britt. AGU, 2005. http://www.agu.org/.
xi News release. NJIT, 2008. http://www.njit.edu/publicinfo/press_releases/release_963.php.
xii News release. NJIT,2008. http://sunearth.gsfc.nasa.gov/ec. http://www.njit.edu/publicinfo/press_releases/release_963.php,
xiii NEO, 2008. http://www.impact.arc.nasa.gov/neo_main.cfm.

xivNear-Earth Asteroid, 433 Eros. Adapted from the NEAR Press Kit. http://nssdc.gsfc.nasa.gov/planetary/text/eros.txt.
xvDennis Gabor. Asteroid Introduction, 2008. http://www.solarviews.com/eng/asteroid.htm.
xviApollo 11, 1969. http://www.kidport.com/RefLib/Science/MoonLanding/MoonLanding.htm#The%20Launch.
xviiJ.R.Church. Solar and Lunar Eclipses in 2015/15..ProphecyintheNews,2008. http://www.treeoflife.wan.io/NTChII/SabbaticalYears.htm.
xviii Mark Bitz. El Shaddai Ministries, 2008. http://www.elshaddaiministries.us/.
xixDr. Joe VanKoevering. Unveiling the Man of Sin. God's News Publishing, 2007.
xxDivision of the Worlds in Islam. Wikipedia, 2007. http://en.wikipedia.org/wiki/Dar_al-Islam#Dar_al-Harb.
xxiPopular Issues, 2007. http://www.allaboutpopularissues.org/12th-imam,12-07-07.
xxiiJamkaran. Wikipedia, 2007. http://en.wikipedia.org/wiki/Jamkaran.
xxiiiDr. David Reagan. Anti-Semitism. Lamplighter, September/October, 2007. Lamb and Lion Ministries. http://www.lamblion.com/pdf/2007/Lamplighter_SepOct_Anti-Semitism.pdf
xxivEncyclopedia Judaica. 1996. 1415.
xxvSabbath Reading. Hebcal Interactive Jewish calendar. http://www.hebcal.com/.